HAYNES MAX POWER Fiat

punto

The definitive guide to **modifying**
by **Bob Jex** & **Em Willmott**

HAYNES MAX POWER Fiat

punto

The definitive guide to modifying
by Bob Jex & Em Willmott

ISBN 1 84425 084 9

Printed by **J H Haynes & Co Ltd,**
Sparkford, Yeovil, Somerset BA22 7JJ, UK.

Tel: 01963 442030 Fax: 01963 440001
Int. tel: +44 1963 442030 Fax: +44 1963 440001
E-mail: sales@haynes.co.uk
Web site: www.haynes.co.uk

Haynes North America, Inc
861 Lawrence Drive, Newbury Park, California 91320, USA

Editions Haynes
4, Rue de l'Abreuvoir
92415 COURBEVOIE CEDEX, France

Haynes Publishing Nordiska AB
Box 1504, 751 45 UPPSALA, Sweden

It wasn't my idea guv'nor!

1 Advice on safety procedures and precautions is contained throughout this manual, and more specifically on page 186. You are strongly recommended to note these comments, and to pay close attention to any instructions that may be given by the parts supplier.

2 J H Haynes recommends that vehicle customisation should only be undertaken by individuals with experience of vehicle mechanics; if you are unsure as to how to go about the customisation, advice should be sought from a competent and experienced individual. Any queries regarding customisation should be addressed to the product manufacturer concerned, and not to J H Haynes, nor the vehicle manufacturer.

3 The instructions in this manual are followed at the risk of the reader who remains fully and solely responsible for the safety, roadworthiness and legality of his/her vehicle. Thus J H Haynes are giving only non-specific advice in this respect.

4 When modifying a car it is important to bear in mind the legal responsibilities placed on the owners, driver and modifiers of cars, including, but not limited to, the Road Traffic Act 1988. IN PARTICULAR, IT IS AN OFFENCE TO DRIVE ON A PUBLIC ROAD A VEHICLE WHICH IS NOT INSURED OR WHICH DOES NOT COMPLY WITH THE CONSTRUCTION AND USE REGULATIONS, OR WHICH IS DANGEROUS AND MAY CAUSE INJURY TO ANY PERSON, OR WHICH DOES NOT HOLD A CURRENT MOT CERTIFICATE OR DISPLAY A VALID TAX DISC.

5 The safety of any alteration and its compliance with construction and use regulations should be checked before a modified vehicle is sold as it may be an offence to sell a vehicle which is not roadworthy.

6 Any advice provided is correct to the best of our knowledge at the time of publication, but the reader should pay particular attention to any changes of specification to the vehicles, or parts, which can occur without notice.

7 Alterations to vehicles should be disclosed to insurers and licensing authorities, and legal advice taken from the police, vehicle testing centres, or appropriate regulatory bodies.

8 The vehicle has been chosen for this project as it is one of those most widely customised by its owners, and readers should not assume that the vehicle manufacturers have given their approval to the modifications.

9 Neither J H Haynes nor the manufacturers give any warranty as to the safety of a vehicle after alterations, such as those contained in this book, have been made. J H Haynes will not accept liability for any economic loss, damage to property or death and personal injury arising from use of this manual other than in respect of injury or death resulting directly from J H Haynes' negligence.

Contents

Haynes
Max Power

Buyer's guide

Insurance

01

02

03

08

Suspension

09

Brakes

10

Interiors

Contents

Security

04

Body styling

05

Lights & bulbs

06

Wheels & tyres

07

11

12

13

14

ICE

Engines

Exhausts

Reference

Haynes Max Power

What's that then?

Haynes Publishing have, for more than forty years, been helping people keep their cars on the roads in countries all over the world by publishing maintenance manuals. Chances are you've either got one of them yourself or you know somebody who has.

"Lights & bulbs" includes fitting high-power blue headlight bulbs, side repeaters, etc.

Before

After

Remember what it feels like on your birthday, or at Christmas, when you're faced by a pile of pressies? So do we, that gnawing feeling in your gut, what's in them? What did I get? Take that feeling and multiply it by twelve, that's how we felt when we started this project. When we decided that it was time to try something new, we couldn't wait. Because the same theories apply to modifying your car as servicing it, we reckoned we'd better get on and do it ourselves. We don't pay other people to do it for us, and we get the same dodgy instructions with kit as everybody else.

So if you've ever wondered how to fit a universal door mirror properly, smooth a tailgate or just bolt a seat in, this book is for you.

We've picked up a skip full of tips along the way, and they're all here for you to use. We haven't tried to set any trends, but we've covered every possible process we think you'll need. So where we've tinted a front door window, the same rules apply to a rear one, job done.

If you look in the magazines and want some of that, join us, 'cos so do we, and we'll show you how to get it.

Keeping it real

Modifying a car is not without its problems in the 'real world', as opposed to the seemingly fantasy world of the glossy mags. For instance, it's pretty silly to spend hours fitting illegal window tints or smoked lights if you get pulled the first time you're out

afterwards. Of course, you can get pulled for all sorts of reasons (and just driving a modified car is reason enough sometimes), but keeping the car actually legal is one of the 'hidden' challenges with modifying. Throughout the book, our tips should give all the help you need to at least appear to be on the right side of the law. The annual MOT test is another favourite time for your mods to get panned, and again, we aim to give you all the help necessary to ensure at least that what you've changed doesn't lead to a fail.

Security is another major issue with a tweaked motor, and the perils of insurance cannot be taken lightly, either. We aim to give down-to-earth advice to help you keep the car in the first place, and to help you in not upsetting your insurers too much if the worst happens.

A word about fashion

In producing this book, we're aware that fashions change. What we show being fitted to our car might well be hideously out of date in 6 months time, or might not be your thing in the first place! Also, some of the stuff we've acquired from our various suppliers may no longer be available by the time you read this. We hope that, despite this, our approach of showing you step-by-step how to fit the various parts will mean that, even if the parts change slightly, the procedures we show for fitting will still be valid.

Our main project car was 1998 Fiat Punto Sporting 16v.

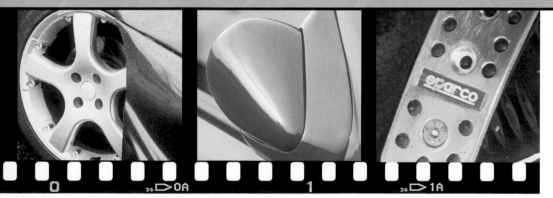

"Wheels & tyres" takes a detailed look at all the options.

"Body styling" shows you how to fit universal mirrors to full body kits.

"Interiors" includes seats, painting trim, gear knobs and loads more.

Spirito di moddo

When you think about it, there aren't many Italian car makes around in the UK, and the largest one, Fiat, only has one model that anyone ever modifies - the Punto. Still, it's one more than Rover. Rarity brings instant cred on the modifying scene.

The Punto landed on our shores in March 1994, as the replacement for the Uno. Italians are well-known champions of style (a certain Mr Beckham would've fitted right in), and the Giugiaro-styled Punto is distinctive and modern, with a look that's still fresh today. Doesn't mean we can't improve things, though! The Punto's loyal following means there's a decent range of bodykits, offering plenty of possibilities in toughening the stance - choose from authentic-sounding Italian names like Cadamuro,

Forza, Abarth, and, er… Beast. It's not the easiest car to get big rims on - if this matters to you, look elsewhere. Luckily, the Punto really suits the Euro-look style of sub-17-inch wheels and slammed suspension.

What's the Italian for boy racer? No, I don't know either. Maybe they don't have 'em in Italy - everyone drives the same way (flippin'

fast). Anyway, speedy spaghetti-munchers are well-served by the Punto Sporting (revvy engine, only ever seems to come in bright yellow) or the fire-breathing GT Turbo (packing 130-odd bhp standard, tuneable to over 200). Even a more basic Punto really does have some "spirito", with go-kart handling and zippy engines making it feel faster than it actually is. Why don't we see more at the cruises? After all, Puntos (unlike Fiats of old, and all Novas) don't rust.

How do you follow-up a Punto? Well, the 1999-on Mk 2 Punto's catching on, so maybe the answer's a simple one. For now, the Mk 1's where it's at for the style-conscious who want something just a bit different. And isn't that what modding's all about?

Buyer's guide

What to buy

The main reason for buying a Punto, of course, is the styling. Like a sharp Italian suit, the Punto's lines are still in fashion - sure, they improved it with the Mk 2 facelift, but have you seen the Mk 3? Yikes. Providing you can resist the GT Turbo, insurance is sensible, with even the fun-to-drive Sporting sitting pretty in Group 7. Loads of room inside, it's pretty well screwed together, and Fiat have finally banished the rust demon.

Any bad news, then? Well, the ride's a bit harsh, and slamming it won't make it any better. It looks stylish on the outside, but inside, it's John Major's favourite colour - we're talking www.seaofgrey.com here (not a real website - I hope). Punto 5-doors are a big no-no style-wise, and there's also no excuse for buying an oil-burner. Spirito di diesel? I think not. The Cabrio's doubtless popular with those of the female persuasion, mostly because it looks like a pram.

Keeping it real

At the budget end of the Punto range, what do we get? Well, to start with, it's all about numbers - as in the 55, 60, 75, 85 and 90. These all roughly tell you how many bhp you can expect your Punto to be packing (and obviously, what your insurance is going to cost).

The lowest of all Puntos is the 1.1 litre 55, which comes in S, SX and EL flavours. The S has no toys, the SX at least gives you electric windows, central locking and a rev counter, while the EL has all this and a 6-speed gearbox. Why six speeds with only 55 horses? You'd better enjoy gearchanging, that's all. Insurance is cheap as chips, in Group 3.

The 60 replaced the 55 in May '97, and you're getting a more-modern 1.2 litre engine for your money. Otherwise, the deal's about the same, and insurance is still Group 3. One to avoid, unless gearchanging gets you down, is the (bo) Selecta, which has a CVT "rubber-band" auto box. The Punto 75 gets its extra 15 horses from multi-point injection, and comes in SX and ELX trim levels (the ELX is the luxury spec, with electric sunroof, front fogs and remote locking). The extra power costs you in insurance, with the 75s in Group 5 or 6. An 85 model has a revvy 16-valve 1.2 litre motor with (you guessed it) 85 bhp, and sits in Group 6, while a 90 model has a 1.6 engine and it's Group 7.

Planning on fitting some large rims? Then you'll need power steering, and for the most part it's only fitted to 85s and 90s upwards (and - whisper it - the diesels).

To sum up - go for a 60 SX if you want to save on insurance (and it's usefully quicker than a 55). Can't quite see the point going for a 75, 85 or 90, when virtually the same insurance money will buy you a Sporting, but then a non-Sporting Punto might be in better nick...

Very sporting of 'em

For something a little sportier, it's gotta be the Sporting - available as the '90 Sporting' to 1997, with a 90-brake 1.6 litre motor, and after that, with a 1.2 litre 16-valver (85 bhp). Only available as a 3-door, often (but not always) in yellow, it's the sports bargain of the range, with Group 7 insurance and a full equipment spec. Sure, a GT would eat one up and spit out the bits, but that's another 7 groups higher. Some people prefer splashing the cash on the car, rather than handing it all to Mr Insurance every year. Your call.

Cheap insurance is for wimps

The GT Turbo is obviously the Daddy, and definitely one for the enthusiasts. Typically terrific turbo thrust throughout, and especially quick when modded. If Group 14 insurance doesn't scare you off, go for it. It's the ultimate Punto-sized thrill, with a 1.4 litre 8-valve turbo engine hoofing out around 130 bhp, it needs the all-round discs and ABS. And new front tyres every other month, probably...

Diesel? If you must...

Awesome fuel economy's hardly very cool, and there's no getting away from the tickover rattle, but hang on - there could be more to this diesel thing than you think. If it doesn't say 'TD' in the advert, you could be looking at a snail-like non-turbo diesel Punto, which no young person should have to suffer driving. But a turbo-diesel could be another matter. Though a TD 70's still only good for around 70 bhp, diesels are all about torque - midrange muscle which slings you down the road. Give one a try. Still Group 5 or 6 for insurance, which is nearly Sporting territory.

Hairdressers only

Finally, there's the drop-top Cabriolet model, available with the 1.6 litre '90' motor, or later with the 1.2 litre 16-valve '85' unit (which might not mess your hair up as much). Very nice. Lovely. Any other comments we might make about these models would have too-sexist overtones, so we'll leave it there.

Don't buy a **dog**

No-one's accusing the Punto of being a girly car, but they are popular with those of the female persuasion. If you can find a one-lady-owner Punto, used only as a second car, you could be in for a major bargain.

With the Punto, Fiat have at last proved they can build a rust-free car, and in general, build quality is pretty solid. So nothing ever goes wrong? Don't be silly. One thing to check early on is whether there's a Fiat dealer anywhere near you - they're getting very thin on the ground, and you're bound to need spares sometime.

Check that the bonnet release works, as they're prone to failing - and while you're under there, check for signs of head gasket failure, which is apparently increasingly common (water on the dipstick, oily sludge in the coolant). Inside the car, if the heater matrix fails, it leaks water onto the engine management ECU, which doesn't do it any good (anything up to complete failure).

If your chosen Punto has an electric sunroof, check very carefully it works - they're a known failure point, and Fiat dealers want £600 to fit a new one. All except the earliest Puntos have a 'red key' immobiliser, and you should be handed the red master key along with all the others - if not, walk away. Any spare keys should start the engine as well as open the doors. Wear in the rear tyres (or instability on corners) might mean the rear suspension arm bushes are worn (one source reckons they only last about 45 000 miles), and similar problems/knocking noises from the front could be the front wishbones going the same way (60 000 miles).

On the test drive, make sure you're happy with how the clutch works, as models with a hydraulic clutch can suffer fluid leaks. Ask the seller if there's ever been any problem with the brakes - seems there have been cases of sudden brake failure, followed by everything going back to normal (and a suggestion that Fiat dealers are replacing brake master cylinders if customers complain). Any misfiring or overheating, and we're back to that head gasket again, while any stalling (not caused by your bad driving) could indicate engine management problems. On a GT, if you're unhappy with anything, either leave it alone or get it professionally checked over - big bills could be around the corner. Buying a GT with no service history could be a giant leap into the unknown. We don't advise it.

All Puntos have a camshaft drivebelt (cambelt, or timing belt) which is made of reinforced rubber. The belt deteriorates with age, and for safety's sake, a new one should be fitted every 3 years or 36 000 miles, especially if the engine gets a regular caning. If the belt snaps, the engine could be wrecked. Finished. Ruined. Knackered. It's not too bad a DIY job if you're confident under the hood, or budget for a garage bill around the £80 mark. Ask for a new tensioner/pulleys at the same time.

General stuff

Usually, it's far better to buy your Punto privately, as long as you know what you're doing. Dealers have to make a living, but sometimes all you'll get for the extra money is a full valet and some degree of comeback if the car's a hound. Buying privately, you get to meet the owner, gaining you valuable clues about how the car's been treated.

Everyone's nervous when buying a car, but don't ignore your 'gut feelings' at first sight, or when meeting the owner. Don't make the mistake of deciding to buy the car *before you've even seen it* - too many people make up their minds before setting out, and blindly ignore all the warning signs. Remember, there *are* other cars, and you *can* walk away! Think of a good excuse before you set out.

Take someone who 'knows a bit about cars' along with you - preferably, try and find someone who's either got a Punto, or who's had one in the past.

Never buy a car in the dark, or when it's raining. If you do have to view any car in these conditions, agree not to hand over any major money until you've seen it in daylight, and when the paintwork's dry (dull, faded paint, or metallic paint that's lost its lacquer, will appear to be shiny in the rain).

Check the mileages and dates shown on the receipts and MoTs follow a pattern indicating normal use, with no gaps in the dates, and no sudden drop in the mileage between MoTs (which might suggest 'clocking'). If you're presented with a sheaf of paperwork, it's worth going through it - maybe the car's had a history of problems, or maybe it's just had some nice new parts fitted (like a clutch, starter motor or alternator, for instance).

Check the chassis number (VIN number) and engine number on the registration document and on the car. Any sign of welding near one of these numbers is suspicious - to disguise the real number, a thief will run a line of weld over the old number, grind it flat, then stamp in a new number. Other scams include cutting the section of bodywork with the numbers on from another car, then cutting and welding this section into place. The VIN plate is

Tricks 'n' tips

Tyres can be a giveaway to a car maintained on a shoestring - four different makes of tyre, especially cheap brands, can indicate a penny-pinching attitude which won't have done the rest of the car any favours.

The VIN number is stamped into the floor next to the driver's seat . . .

. . . and also appears on this plate under the bonnet.

Full service history (fsh)

Is there any service history? If so, this is good, but study the service book carefully:

a *Which garage has done the servicing? Is it a proper dealer, or a backstreet bodger? Do you know the garage, and if so, would you use it?*

b *Do the mileages show a nice even progression, or are there huge gaps? Check the dates too.*

c *Does it look as if the stamps are authentic? Do the oldest ones look old, or could this 'service history' have been created last week, to make the car look good?*

d *When was the last service, and what exactly was carried out? When was the cambelt last changed? Has the owner got receipts for any of this servicing work?*

One sign of a genuine car is a good batch of old MOTs, and as many receipts as possible - even if they're for fairly irrelevant things like tyres.

located under the bonnet, behind the driver's-side headlight, and the number is also stamped into the floor next to the driver's seat (lift the plastic flap in the carpet).

The engine number is stamped into the front of the engine block, at the transmission end - shouldn't be difficult to spot. If the number's been removed, or if there's anything suspicious about it, you could be buying trouble.

Check the registration document (V5) very carefully - all the details should match the car. Never buy a car without seeing the V5 - accept no excuses on this point. If buying privately, make sure it's definitely the owner's name and address printed on it - if not, be very careful! If buying from a dealer, note the name and address, and try to contact the previous owner to confirm mileage, etc, before handing over more than a deposit. The car shouldn't have had many previous owners - otherwise, it may mean the car is trouble, so checking its owner history is more important.

While the trim on a Punto is quite durable, it should still be obvious whether the car's been abused over a long period, or whether the mileage showing is genuine or not (shiny steering wheels, worn carpets and pedals are a good place to start checking if you're suspicious). Okay, so you may be planning to junk most of the interior at some point, but why should you pay over the odds for a tat car which the owner hasn't given a stuff about?

Although you may feel a bit stupid doing it, check simple things too, like making sure the windows and sunroof open and shut, and that all the doors and tailgate can be locked (if a lock's been replaced, ask why). Check all the basic electrical equipment - lights, front and rear wipers, heated rear window, heater fan; it's amazing how often these things are taken for granted by buyers! If your chosen Punto already has alloys fitted, does it have locking wheel bolts? Where's the key? What about the code and removal tools for the stereo?

Is the catalytic converter ('cat') working? This is a wickedly expensive part to replace - the best way to ensure at least one year's grace is to only buy a car with a full MoT (the cat is checked during the emissions test). Many Punto modifiers remove the cat altogether (by fitting a de-cat pipe), which is great for performance, but means the car's illegal to use on the road.

Look closer

Don't take anything at face value. Even a fully-stamped service book only tells half the story of how your chosen Punto has been treated. Does the owner look bright enough to even know what a dipstick is, never mind how to check the oil level between services?

Check for signs of accident damage, especially at the front end (and even more so, on the sporty models). Ask if it's ever been in a shunt - if the seller says no, but there's paint overspray under the bonnet, what's going on? Also check for paint overspray on the window rubbers, light units and bumpers/trim. Look at the car side-on - are there any mis-matched panels? With the bonnet open, check that the headlight rear shells are the same colour - mis-matched or new-looking ones merit an explanation from the seller. Does the front number plate carry details of the supplying garage, like the back one? If not, why has a new plate been fitted?

Check the glass (and even the head and tail lights) for etched-in registration numbers - are they all the same, and does it match the car's actual registration? Later Puntos have the VIN etched on the glass - does it match the logbook? A windscreen could've been innocently replaced, but new side glass indicates a break-in at least - is the car a 'stolen/recovered' (joyridden) example? Find the chassis and engine numbers, as described earlier in this Section, and satisfy yourself that they're genuine - check them against the registration document. An HPI check (or similar) is worthwhile, but even this won't tell you everything. If you're in doubt, or if the

answers to your questions don't ring true, walk away. Make any excuse you like.

The Punto from February 1995 has a decent immobiliser as standard, but there's no harm fitting a good ultrasonic alarm on top (if it hasn't already got one) - might even be worth a bit of insurance discount. Make sure that any aftermarket alarm actually works, that it looks properly installed, with no stray wires hanging out, and that you get the Thatcham certificate or other paperwork to go with it. If possible, it's worth finding out exactly how it's been wired in - if it goes wrong later, you could be stranded with no chance of disabling the system to get you home.

Model history

Note: *As usual, there are plenty of "special edition" Punto models. Don't pay over the odds for a special edition, unless it's really got some extra kit you actually want.*

March 1994 (L reg) - Punto range introduced in the UK. 3-door and 5-door hatchbacks, 1.1 (55), 1.2 (75), 1.4 GT Turbo and 1.7 litre TD (turbo diesel). Trim levels - S, SX, ELX. SX has central locking, electric windows; ELX adds remote locking, front fogs, electric sunroof; GT has alloys, side skirts, headlight washers, electric mirrors, alarm/immobiliser.

August 1994 (M reg) - 55 EL introduced, with 6-speed gearbox. 60 SX Selecta introduced, with CVT automatic transmission. 1.6 litre '90' models launched, including Punto Cabriolet with electric hood, immobiliser.

February 1995 (M reg) - Immobiliser and VIN number window etching standard across the range. ELX, GT and Cabrio gain driver's airbag.

June 1995 (M reg) - 1.6 litre 90 Sporting introduced, similar to GT, but with 90 bhp engine, equipment similar to ELX. 1.7 litre D S introduced, with non-turbo diesel engine (56 bhp).

November 1996 (P reg) - Non-turbo diesel replaced by TD 60S, a low-pressure turbo model with 63 bhp.

June 1997 (P reg) - Revised range - 1.1 litre 55 models replaced by 1.2 litre 8-valve 60 (single-point injection). 1.2 litre 75 models continue with multi-point injection. 1.6 litre 90 models replaced by 1.2 litre 16-valve 85. Cosmetic changes, minor suspension and steering revisions. Sporting gets GT alloys and side skirts, GT gains anodised alloys. Airbags and air conditioning more widely available across the range.

March 1998 (R reg) - Punto 75 models replaced by 1.2 litre 16-valve 85 versions, 85 ELX gains alloy wheels.

June 1998 (R reg) - Limited edition 'Team' models introduced, based on 60 S and TD 60S - sunroof and SX instrumentation.

July 1999 (T reg) - Last of the Punto 60 S models now have power steering and alloys as standard.

October 1999 - Punto Mk 1 production ends - replaced by Mk 2 models.

Performance figures

	0-60 (sec)	Top speed (mph)
55 S, SX	14.8	95
60 S, SX	12.6	94
75 SX	12.5	105
85 ELX and Sporting	11.5	108
90 Sporting	10.6	108
GT Turbo	8.1	127
TD 60S	16.8	96
TD 70S	13.7	99

Insurance
A necessary evil

Ah, insurance - loads of money, and all you get is a piece of paper you're not supposed to use! Of course, you must have insurance - you're illegal on the road without it, and you won't be able to get the car taxed, either. If you're ever caught driving without insurance, you'll have great trouble ever getting insurance again - insurance companies regard this offence nearly as seriously as drink-driving, so don't do it!

The way insurance companies work out premiums and assess risks is a mystery to most of us. In general, the smaller the engine you have in your Punto, the less you'll pay. However, if one company's had a lot of claims on Puntos in the past, the GT factor might 'unfairly' influence the premiums of lesser Puntos, too (this is why it's important to shop around). An 'insurance-friendly' Sporting should be a good bet for a sensible premium, but remember that insurance companies aren't stupid - if you swap in that turbo engine and turn your Sporting into a GT-alike, they may well 'load' the premium to GT level (and that's Group 14). Insurance is a game you can't win, but you must play.

If your annual premium seems like the national debt of a small African country (and whose isn't!), always ring as many brokers and get as many quotes as you possibly can. Yes, there's loads better ways to spend an evening/afternoon than answering the same twenty questions over and over again, but you never know what the next quote will be. A few extra minutes spent on the phone (or on the 'net) once a year may result in an extra few hundred quid in your back pocket. Well, you live in hope don't you!

With modified cars, insurance becomes even more of a problem. By putting on all the alloys, trick body kits, nice interiors, big ICE, you're making the car much more of a target for thieves (yes, ok, we know you know this). The point is, the insurance companies know this too, and they don't want to be paying out for the car, plus all the money you've spent on it, should it go missing. There is a temptation 'not to tell the insurance' about the mods you've

Tricks 'n' tips

When ringing for quotes, watch your language. Arguing with the bloke/girl on the other end will always get you a higher quote, even if it makes you feel better. Also, don't say anything if you get put on hold. Some companies will put you on speaker - if you're trying to pull a fast one and they then catch you giggling or bragging to your mates, it's game over.

made. Let's deal with this right now. Our experience has been that, while it can be painful, honesty is best. Generally, the insurance company line is: '...thanks for telling us - we won't put the car 'up a group' (ie charge you more), but we also won't cover the extra cost of your alloy wheels/body kit/tasty seats in the event of any claim...'. This is fair enough - in other words, if your car goes missing, you get paid out, based on a standard car, minus all the goodies. If you particularly want all the extras covered, you might have a long hard search - most companies only offer 'modified for standard' policies. There are specialist insurers who are more friendly towards fully-loaded cars, but even they won't actually cover the cost of replacement goodies.

What type of cover, Sir?

For most of us, cost means there's only one option - TPF&T (third party, fire and theft). Fully-comp insurance is an unattainable dream for most people until they reach the 'magic' age of 25, but what's the real story?

Third Party only

The most basic cover you can get. Basically covers you for damage to other people's cars or property, and for personal injury claims. Virtually no cover for your own stuff, beyond what you get if you take the optional 'legal protection' cover.

Third Party, Fire and Theft

As above, with cover for fire and theft, of course! Better, but not much better. This is really only cover in the event of a 'total loss', if your car goes missing or goes up in smoke. Still no cover for your car if you stack it into a tree, or if someone breaks in and pinches your stereo (check your policy small-print).

Fully-comprehensive

In theory at least, covers you for any loss or damage. Will cover the cost of repairing or replacing your car, often with discounted windscreen cover and other benefits. If you lose control of the car on an icy road (arguably, not your fault) you get paid. If someone pinches your wheels and drops the car on the floor, you get paid - at least for the damage done to the underside, and for standard wheels and tyres. Most policies include provision of a hire car after a shunt, which is pretty useful. Some offer cheap breakdown cover packages in with the main policy. With a fully-comp policy, you can 'protect' your no-claims bonus for a small fee so you don't automatically lose all those hard-earned years' worth of discount if you prang it (generally, you can only do this on fully-comp).

All this extra cover costs, obviously, but how much? You might be surprised what the actual difference is. Think about it, anyway - it's got to be worth a couple of hundred quid more to go fully-comp, if your car's worth into four figures, surely?

Valuing your car

When your insurance pays out in the event of a total loss or write-off, they base their offer on the current market value of an identical standard model to yours (less your excess). The only way you'll get more than the average amount is to prove your Punto is in above-average nick (with photos?) or that the mileage was especially low for the year.

With this in mind, don't bother over-valuing your Punto in the hope you'll get more in the event of a claim - you won't! The only way to do this is to seek out an 'agreed-value' deal, which you can usually only get on classic-car policies (with these, the car's value is agreed in advance between you, not worked out later by the company with you having no say in it). By over-valuing your Punto, you could be increasing your premium without gaining any benefit - sound smart to you?

Equally though, don't under-value, in the hope you'll get a reduction in premium. You won't, and if there's a total loss claim, you won't get any more than your under-valued amount, no matter how loudly you complain.

Work on what you paid for the car, backed up with the sort of prices you see for similar cars in the ads (or use a secondhand car price guide). Add no more than 10% for the sake of optimism, and that's it.

Your car? Or your Dad's?

Insurance really costs when you're the wrong side of 25. Ever been tempted to tell your insurance that your full-on sorted Punto belongs to your Dad (old insurance-friendly person), then get him to insure it, with you as a named driver? Oh dear. This idea (known as 'fronting') is so old, it's grown a long white beard. And it sucks, too. First of all, insurance companies aren't stupid. They know your Dad (or your Mum, or old Uncle Bert) isn't likely to be running around in a kid's pocket-rocket, and they treat any 'named driver' application with great suspicion. Even if they do take your money, don't imagine they've been suckered. In the event of a claim, they'll look into everything very carefully, and will ask lots of awkward questions. If you get caught out in the lie, they've taken your money, and you've got no insurance - who's been suckered now?

This dubious practice also does you no favours in future years. All the time you're living the lie, you're not building up any no-claims bonus of your own - you're just delaying the pain 'til later, and without having real cover in the meantime.

'Legit' ways to limit your premium

If you do enough ringing around for quotes, you'll soon learn what the 'right answers' to some of the questions are - even if you can't actually give them (don't tell lies to your insurance company). Mind you, with a little thought, you can start to play their game and win - try these:

Volunteer to increase your excess. The 'excess' is put there to stop people claiming for piddling little amounts - when they pay out, it's always the repair/replacement cost minus whatever the 'excess' is. So, for instance, if you've got a £200 theft excess, it means you'll automatically get £200 less than the agreed value of your car, should it be stolen. Most policies have 'compulsory' excess amounts, which you can do nothing about. By increasing excesses voluntarily, you're limiting the amount you'll get still further. Insurance companies like this, and should reduce your premium in return - but this only goes so far, so ask what the effect of different voluntary excesses will be. Don't increase your excess too far, or you'll get paid nowt if you claim!

Limit your mileage. Most companies offer a small discount if you only cover a small annual mileage. To get any meaningful reduction, the mileage has to be a lot less than 10,000 per year. Few companies, though, ever ask what the car's current mileage is - so how are they gonna know if you've gone over your self-imposed limit?

Make yourself the only driver. Pretty self-explanatory. The more people who drive your car, the greater the risk to the company, and a car's owner will always drive more carefully (it's their money that bought it) than any named driver. If you've built up 2 years' worth of no-claims, but your partner hasn't, putting them on your insurance will bump it up, due to their relative inexperience

Get a garage - and use it. Where you park can have a big effect on your premium. Parking it on the street is the worst. Park off the road (on a driveway) when you're at home. The best thing is to have a garage of your own (don't pretend you use your Dad's garage) - see if you can rent one locally, even if it means walking a few hundred yards. If you're a student living away from home, tell your company where the car will be parked during term-time - if you're at Uni in London, this is a bigger risk than living at home 'in the country', and vice-versa.

Fit an approved alarm or immobiliser. See if you can get a list from your company of all their approved security devices, and fit whatever you can afford. Not all companies approve the same kit, so it might even be worth contacting more than one company for advice. Any device with a Thatcham or Sold Secure rating should be recognised. In some cases, the discounts offered are not that great any more - but an alarm is still a nice way to get peace of mind.

Build up your no-claims bonus. You'll only do this by owning and insuring a car in your own name, and then not making any claims. Simple really. One rather immoral (but not actually illegal) dodge is to buy an old banger, insure it cheap, then never drive it. You'll need to keep it fully road-legal (with tax, MOT) if you park it on the road. For every year you do this, you'll build up another year of NCB.

Hang onto your no-claims bonus. Obviously, the less you claim, the less your insurance will cost. If something happens to your car, don't be in too big a hurry to make a claim before you've thought it all through. How much will it cost to fix? How much is your excess? How much will your renewal premium be, next year? If you have a big enough accident which you're sure isn't your fault, ring your company, but make it quite clear you're not claiming yet - just informing them of the accident. It should be down to the other driver's insurance to pay. You don't always lose all your no-claims, either, even if it was your fault - depends how many years you've built up. Once you've got a few years, ask whether you can 'protect' your no-claims.

Avoid speed cameras and The Law. Yes, okay, easier said than done! But anything less than a clean licence is not good from the insurance perspective. One SP30 won't hurt much, but the second strike will, so take it easy. Don't get caught on traffic-light cameras, either - just one is a major no-no.

Insurance-friendly mods?

Insurers don't like any changes from standard, but some things you'll do are worse from their viewpoint than others. The guidelines below are just that - for guidance. No two companies will have the same outlook, and your own circumstances will play a big part too.

Golden Rule Number One: Before you spend huge money modifying the car, ring your insurance, and ask them how it will affect things.

Golden Rule Number Two: If in doubt, declare everything. Insurance companies are legally entitled to dispute any claim if the car is found to be non-standard in any way.

Body mods – Even a tiny rear spoiler could be classed as a 'bodykit' (yes, it's daft, but that's how it is). Anything which alters the exterior appearance should be declared. As long as the mods don't include a radical full-on bodykit, the jump in premium should be fairly small. Any genuine Fiat add-ons (GT side skirts) might not cost at all - bonus.

Brakes – The companies view brake mods as tampering with safety-related kit, and modifying the brakes implies that you drive fast and hard. You might get away with standard-sized grooved/drilled discs and pads, but fitting bigger discs and replacement calipers will prove expensive.

Engine mods – 'Mild' mods such as induction kits and exhausts don't give much more power, so don't generally hurt. But 'chipping' your Punto will lead to drastic rises in premiums, or a complete refusal of cover. With complete engine transplants, you'll be required to give an engineer's report, and to get your wad out.

Interior mods – Don't assume that tarting up the inside won't interest the insurance company. By making any part of the car more attractive, you're also attracting the crims. Cars get trashed for parts, as often as not - and your racing seats and sexy steering wheel could be worth major money. Still, the effect on premiums shouldn't be too great, especially if you've got an approved alarm.

Lights – Change the car's appearance, and are safety-related. You'll probably get asked for lots of details, but as long as you've kept it sensible (and legal, as far as possible), the effect on your wallet shouldn't be too harsh.

Security – Make sure you mention all security stuff - alarms, immobilisers (including mechanical devices), locking wheel nuts, large Alsatian in the back seat… But - don't over-sell the car. Tell the truth, in other words. If you've got a steering wheel lock, do you always fit it? If you didn't when your car went missing, you're in trouble. Don't say you've got a Cat 1 alarm if it really came from Argos, and don't tell them you garage the car at night if it's stuck out in the road.

Suspension – Changes the car's appearance, and is safety-related. Some enlightened companies once took the view that modded suspension helps the car corner better, so it's safer. Drops of only 30 to 40 mm shouldn't mean bigger premiums.

Wheels – Very appearance-altering, and very nickable. At least show some responsibility by fitting some locking nuts/bolts and an approved alarm. Quite likely to attract a low-to-moderate rise in premium, which still won't cover your wheels properly - you could arrange separate cover for your wheels, then at least you'll get paid. Some companies may ask for a photo of the car with the wheels on.

And finally - a new nightmare

Not telling the insurance the whole truth gets a little tricky when you make a claim. If the insurance assessor comes to check your bent/burnt/stolen-and-recovered 'standard' Punto, and finds he's looking at a vehicle fitted with trick alloys/bodykit/radical interior, he's not going to turn a blind eye. Has the car got an MoT? Oh, and did you declare those points on your licence? No? You're then very much at the mercy of your insurer, especially if they can prove any mods contributed to the claim. At best, you'll have a long-drawn-out battle with your insurer to get a part-payout, and at worst they'll just refuse to get involved at all.

One more thing - *be careful what you hit*. If your insurance is declared void, they won't pay out for the repairs to the other car you smacked into, or for the lamp-post you knock down (several hundred quid, actually). And then there's the personal injury claims - if your insurance company disowns you, it'll be you who has to foot the bill. Even sprains and bruises can warrant claims, and more serious injuries can result in claims running into lots of zeroes! Without insurance cover, **you'll** have to pay. Probably for a long, long time. Think about it, and we won't see you in court.

Security

Lock me or lose me

It's a sad fact, but making your car attractive to the opposite sex also tends to attract attention of a less-welcome kind, from less-than-human pond life.

Avoiding trouble

Now come on - you're modifying your car to look cool and to be seen in. Not a problem - but be careful where you choose to show your car off, and who to. Be especially discreet, the nearer you get to home - *turn your system down* before you turn into your road, for instance, or you'll draw unwelcome attention to where that car with the loud stereo's parked at night.

Without being too paranoid, watch for anyone following you home. At night, if the car behind switches its lights off, be worried. If you suspect this is happening, do not drive home - choose well-lit public places until they give up. Believe us - it happens.

If you're going out, think about where you're parking - well-lit and well-populated is good.

Thieves hate light being on them, so don't make it easy by parking somewhere dark - think about this if you park up in daylight, knowing you won't be back 'til late.

Hands up, who doesn't lock their car when they get petrol? Your insurance company has a term for this, and it's 'contributory negligence'. In English, this means you won't get a penny if your car goes missing when you haven't locked it.

If you're lucky enough to have a garage, use it. On up-and-over garage doors, fit extra security like a padlock and ground anchor.

A clever thief will watch your movements and habits over several days before trying your car. Has it got an alarm, and do you always set it? Do you only fit your steering wheel lock when you feel like it? Do you always park in the same place, and is the car hidden from the house or from the road? Don't make his life easier. Ask yourself how you'd nick your car…

A word about your stereo

From the moment you bolt on those nice alloys, it's taken as read that you've also got stereo gear that's worth nicking - and the thieves know it. All the discreet installation in the world isn't going to deter them from finding out what's inside that nice motor.

Please don't advertise your love of ICE around your car. Your nice stereo gear will fit other cars too, and can be ripped out in nothing flat. You may be very proud of your ICE install, but nothing is more of an 'invite' than a huge ICE sticker or sunstrip. If you've fitted one just to look cool, replace it now with something less provocative - seriously. Your set might not actually be very expensive, but you could still lose a side window for advertising something better.

You'll have got a CD player, obviously, but don't leave discs or empty CD cases lying around inside the car. A nice pair of 6x9s in full view on the back shelf is an invite to having your rear window smashed - stealth shelf, anyone? When you're fitting your system, give some thought to the clues you could accidentally leave in plain view. Oxygen-free speaker cable is great stuff, but it's also a bit bright against dark carpets, and is all the clue necessary that you're serious about your tunes. Hide amps and CD changers under your front seats, or in the boot.

Most modern sets are face-off or MASK, so if they've got security features like this, use them - take your faceplate off when you leave the car, and take it with you rather than leaving it in the door pocket or glovebox (the first places a thief will look).

Things that go beep in the night

Unless your insurance company demands it up front, fitting an alarm is something generally done as an after-thought. We know alarms aren't exactly sexy, but don't skimp - an alarm may never be put to the test, but if it is, you'll be glad you spent wisely…

The simplest first step to car security is to fake it. Tacky *'This car is fitted with an alarm'* stickers won't fool anyone, but if you want cheap, just fit a flashing LED. We know it's not the real thing, but everyone else will think you've got a posh alarm. An LED is cheap to buy and easy to fit, and can be rigged to a discreet switch inside the car.

Don't overlook the value of so-called 'manual' immobilisers, such as steering wheel locking bars and gear-to-handbrake lever locks. These can be a worthwhile deterrent - a thief not specifically after your car may move on to an easier target. Some of the items offered may be 'Sold Secure' or Thatcham Cat 3, accolades well worth checking out, since it means they've withstood a full-on brute force attack for a useful length of time.

The only way to combat the more determined thief is to go for a well-specified and intelligently-installed alarm. Immobilisers alone have their place, but sadly, even a pro-fitted immobiliser on its own won't stop someone pinching your wheels, or having it away with the stereo gear. Neither, incidentally, will a cheap alarm - you have to know how the thieves operate to stand any chance defeating them. Any alarm you fit yourself probably won't gain you any insurance discount, but it will give you peace of mind, and DIY means you can do a real trick installation, to make it very hard work for the scum.

Finally, one other scam which you might fall victim to. If you find your alarm is suddenly going off a lot at night, when previously it had been well-behaved, don't ignore the problem. It's an old trick for a thief to deliberately set off your alarm several times, each time hiding round the corner when you come out to investigate, then to wait until the fifth or sixth time when you don't reset it (in disgust), leaving him a clear run. If your alarm does keep false-alarming

without outside assistance, find out the cause quickly, or your neighbours will quickly become 'deaf' to it.

Thatcham categories and meanings:

1 Cat 1. For alarms and electronic immobilisers.

2 Cat 2. For electronic immobilisers only.

3 Cat 2-1. Electronic immobilisers which can be upgraded to Cat 1 alarms later.

4 Cat 3. Mechanical immobilisers, eg snap-off steering wheels, locking wheel bolts, window film, steering wheel locks/covers.

5 Q-class. Tracking devices.

Other alarm features

Two-stage anti-shock - means that the alarm shouldn't go off, just because the neighbour's cat jumps on your car roof, or because Little Johnny punts his football into your car. Alarm will only sound after a major shock, or after repeated shocks are detected.

Anti-tilt - detects any attempt to lift or jack up the car, preventing any attempt to pinch alloys. Very unpopular with thieves, as it makes the alarm very sensitive (much more so than anti-shock). Alarm may sound if car is parked outside in stormy conditions (but not if your suspension's rock-hard!).

Anti-hijack - immobiliser with built-in delay. If your motor gets hijacked, the neanderthals responsible will only get so far down the road before the engine cuts out.

Rolling code - reduces the chance of your alarm remote control signal from being 'grabbed' by special electronic equipment.

Total closure - module which connects to electric windows/sunroof and central locking, which closes all items when alarm is set. Alarms like this often have other nifty features such as remote boot opening.

Pager control - yes, really - your alarm can be set to send a message to your pager (why not your mobile?) if your car gets tampered with.

Current-sensing disable - very useful feature on some cars which have a cooling fan which can cut in after the ignition is switched off. Without this feature, your alarm will be triggered every time you leave it parked after a long run - very annoying.

Volumetric-sensing disable - allows you to manually disable the interior ultrasonics, leaving the rest of the alarm features active. Useful if you want to leave the sunroof open in hot weather - if a fly gets in the car, the alarm would otherwise be going off constantly.

Talking alarms - no, please, please no. Very annoying, and all that'll happen is you'll attract crowds of kids daring each other to set it off again. Unfortunately, these are becoming more popular, with some offering the facility to record your own message!

The knowledge

What people often fail to realise (at least, until it happens to them) is the level of violence and destruction which thieves will employ to get your stuff - this goes way beyond breaking a window.

It comes as a major shock to most people when they discover the serious kinds of tools (weapons) at many professional thieves' disposal, and how brutally your lovingly-polished car will be attacked. Many people think, for instance, that it's their whole car they're after, whereas it's really only the parts they want, and they don't care how they get them (this means that these parts are still attractive, even when fitted to a basic car which has yet to be fully modded). Obviously, taking the whole car then gives the option of hiding it to strip at leisure, but it won't always be the option chosen, and you could wake up one morning to a well-mangled wreck outside.

Attack 1 The first option to any thief is to smash glass - typically, the toughened-glass side windows, which will shatter, unlike the windscreen. Unfortunately for the thief, this makes a loud noise (not good), but is a quick and easy way in. The reason for taking this approach is that a basic car alarm will only go off if the doors are opened (voltage-drop alarm) - provided the doors aren't opened, the alarm won't go off.

Response 1 A more sophisticated alarm will feature shock sensing (which will be set off by the impact on the glass), and better still, ultrasonic sensing, which will be triggered by the brick coming in through the broken window.

Response 2 This kind of attack can also be stopped by applying security film to the inside of the glass, which holds it all together and prevents easy entry.

Attack 2 An alternative to smashing the glass is to pry open the door using a crowbar - this attack involves literally folding open the door's window frame by prising from the top corner. The glass will still shatter, but as long as the door stays shut, a voltage-drop alarm won't be triggered.

Response This method might not be defeated by a shock-sensing alarm, but an ultrasonic unit would pick it up.

Incidentally, another bonus with ultrasonic alarms is that the sensors are visible from outside - and act as a deterrent.

Attack 3 The next line of attack is to disable the alarm. The commonest way to kill the alarm is either to cut the wiring to the alarm itself, or to disconnect the battery, 'safely' hidden away under the bonnet. And just how strong is a bonnet? Not strong enough to resist being crowbarred open, which is exactly what happens.

Response 1 If your alarm has extra pin-switches, be sure to fit one to the bonnet, and fit it in the bonnet channel next to the battery, so that it'll set off the alarm if the bonnet is prised up. Also make sure that the wire to the pin-switch cannot be cut easily though a partly-open bonnet.

Response 2 Make sure that the alarm module is well-hidden, and cannot be got at from underneath the car.

Response 3 Make the alarm power supply connection somewhere less obvious than directly at the battery terminal - any thief who knows his stuff will immediately cut any 'spare' red wires at the battery. Try taking power from the fusebox, or if you must source it under the bonnet, trace the large red battery lead to the starter motor connections, and tap into the power there.

Response 4 Always disguise the new alarm wiring, by using black insulating tape to wrap it to the existing wiring loom. Tidying up in this way also helps to ensure the wires can't get trapped, cut, melted, or accidentally ripped out - any of which could leave you with an alarm siren which won't switch off, or an immobiliser you can't disable.

Response 5 An alarm which has a 'battery back-up' facility is a real kiss of death to the average thief's chances. Even if he's successfully crow-barred your bonnet and snipped the battery connections, the alarm will still go off, powered by a separate battery of its own. A Cat 1 alarm has to have battery back-up.

Fitting a basic LED

All you need for this is a permanent live feed, an earth, a switch if you want to be able to turn it on/off, and the flashing LED itself (very cheap, from any car accessory shop).

An LED draws very little current, so you'll be quite safe tapping into almost any live feed you fancy. If you've wired in your ICE, take a live feed from the permanent (radio memory supply) wire at the back of your head unit, or have a delve into the back of the fusebox with your test light. An earth can easily be tapped again from your head unit, or you can make one almost anywhere on the metal body of the car, by drilling a small hole, fitting a self-tapping screw, then wrapping the bared end of wire around and tightening it.

The best and easiest place to mount an LED is into one of the many blank switches the makers seem to love fitting. The blank switch is easily pried out, and a hole can then be drilled to take the LED (which usually comes in a separate little holder). Feed the LED wiring down behind the dashboard to where you've tapped your live and earth, taking care not to trap it anywhere, nor to accidentally wrap it around any moving parts.

Connect your live to the LED red wire, then rig your earth to one side of the switch, and connect the LED black wire to the other switch terminal. You should now have a switchable LED! Tidy up the wiring, and mount the switch somewhere discreet, but where you can still get at it. Switch on when you leave the car, and it looks as if you've got some sort of alarm - better than nothing!

Wiring basics

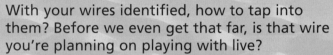

With your wires identified, how to tap into them? Before we even get that far, is that wire you're planning on playing with live?

Switch off the ignition at least - and ideally disconnect the battery before you do anything else. On cars with airbags, don't go tapping into any of the airbag wiring, which is usually bright yellow. With that cleared up, how were you planning on joining the old and new wires together?

Here's our advice:

Soldering - avoids cutting through your chosen wire - strip away a short section of insulation, wrap your new wire around the bared section, then apply solder to secure it. If you're a bit new to soldering, practice on a few offcuts of wire first - it ain't rocket science! Re-insulate the soldered connection afterwards, with tape or heatshrink tube.

Bullet connectors - cut and strip the end of your chosen wire, wrap your new one to it, push both into one half of the bullet and crimp to secure. Connect the other end of your victim wire to the other bullet, and connect together. Always use the 'female' half on any live feed - it'll be safer if you disconnect it than a male bullet, which could touch bare metal and send your motor up in smoke.

Block connectors - so easy to use. Just remember that the wires can come adrift if the screws aren't really tight, and don't get too ambitious about how many wires you can stuff in one hole (block connectors, like bullets, are available in several sizes). Steer clear of connectors like the one below - they're convenient, but they can give rise to problems.

With any of these options, always insulate around your connection - especially when soldering, or you'll be leaving bare metal exposed. Remember that you'll probably be shoving all the wires up into the dark recesses of the under-dash area - by the time the wires are nice and kinked/squashed together, that tiny bit of protruding wire might just touch that bit of metal bodywork, and that'll be a fire...

Fitting an auxiliary fusebox

You'll need plenty of fused live feeds from the battery during the modifying process, for stereo gear, neons, starter buttons - and alarms, and it's always a pain working out where to tap into one. If you make up your own little fusebox, mounted somewhere easy to get at, you'll never have this problem again - and it's easy enough to do.

01 First job is to find a suitable place to mount the fusebox. This may prove a little more difficult than it sounds - we chose to mount ours under the centre of the dash, in front of the centre console. To get where we want to be, the passenger footwell carpet has to come out a bit, so first we prised out this retainer by the glovebox . . .

02 . . . and pulled down this sound-deadening panel.

03 Free the top corner of the carpet by prising off part of the door rubber seal . . .

08 On the other side of the fuse, add on a piece of eight-gauge wire long enough to reach well inside the car. Soldering wires this thick requires a hefty soldering tool - this is a butane-powered one, which laughs this off, and is a very handy little gadget to have around. Again, insulate the soldered joint.

09 Don't connect up to the battery yet - remember, the minute that lead goes on, it's live, and will spark on every bit of metal it touches. Now we're looking for a way to get our heavy red lead into the car, and we've found one, behind this bit of bulkhead insulation (held on by this plastic clip).

10 What we've found is a rubber grommet, and one which isn't even being used for anything - bonus. Prise it out, and make a slit in it . . .

11 . . . big enough to feed the thick wire through, and now the wire's in the car, ready to hook up to our new fusebox.

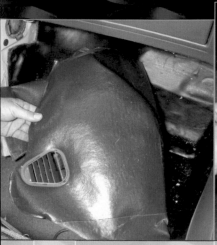

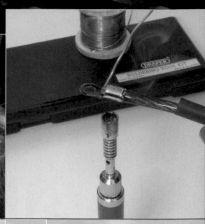

04 . . . then the carpet can be folded back, and unclipped from the centre console - we're in!

05 Next, we tried the fusebox in position, and marked round it on the thick sound-deadening . . .

06 . . . which then received our attention with the knife, to give a nice area of bare metal. Now we know where it's all going, it's time to start thinking about the wiring.

07 Take one heavy-duty in-line fuse holder, and add a ring terminal large enough to go on the battery terminal (solder it on for extra security, and insulate the joint with tape or heat-shrink). You'll need a pretty large fuse in there - eight-gauge wire should be able to handle a total of 30 amps at least, but check with your supplier.

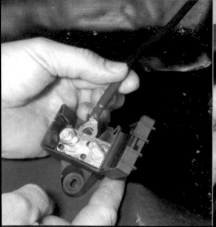

12 Inside the car, we've now crimped a ring terminal onto our live feed, ready to connect to the first component of our fusebox install - this rather neat junction box. The junction box takes in our thick live feed on one screw terminal, and allows us to split it six ways, to connect to the six terminals on our 'box.

13 With the main feed attached, the next job is making up six short lengths of wire, which go between the junction box and fusebox - each one slips over the other junction box terminal, and all six are secured with the nut.

14 With double-sided tape holding the junction box on the floor, this part of the install's looking pretty tidy. The six wires for the fusebox have been loomed together with some plastic spiral, but you could use tape.

15 All that's left is to connect up the six wires, then drill and screw the fusebox into place. Connect up the battery to complete the job. Now whenever you need a live feed, hook up to the fusebox, slip in a fuse of the correct rating, and you're done.

Alarm fitting

If your Punto already has a decent aftermarket alarm on it, don't mess with it. Otherwise, be prepared for some nasty surprises when you dive behind the dash. How the heck have they wired this in? Will chopping that wire mean the car won't start? If it looks a mess behind there, it's best to leave it - and then hope it never goes wrong, or you'll have to suss it all out anyway.

If your Punto is still a virgin in the aftermarket alarm sense, things are a bit easier. The alarm we've chosen to fit is a MicroScan, which, whilst it isn't a Clifford, still offers a decent level of protection, and a useful array of features for a sensible price. When it goes off, it actually sounds like a Clifford - result!

As with everything else in this book, remember that we're showing you just how this *particular* alarm is fitted. All the same, whatever alarm you fit, it'll still be useful to pick out the fitting principles and tips. Always refer to the instructions which come with your alarm, and don't go joining the red wire to the yellow wire, just because WE say so…

01 Disconnect the battery negative lead, and move the lead away from the battery, or you'll be blowing fuses and your new alarm will go mental the minute it's rigged up.

02 Decide where you're going to mount the alarm/siren. Choose somewhere not easily reached from underneath, for a start, and if you can, pick a location away from where you'll be topping up washers, oil or coolant - fluids and alarm modules don't mix. The only spot on our Punto was on the passenger's-side inner wing.

03 Mark the mounting hole positions through the bracket with some white paint or marker pen . . .

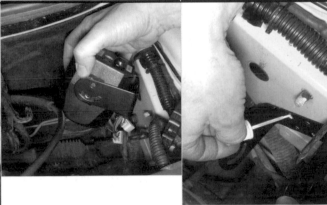

>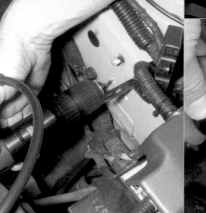

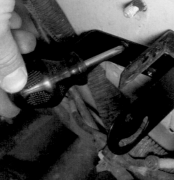

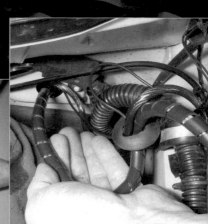

04 . . . then work a drill in there (this isn't easy, but you can buy 'snake' flexible drive attachments for drilling into awkward corners) . . .

05 . . . and screw that bracket into place.

06 Well, that was the easy bit - now there's wires to play with. Most of them need to go through into the car, but not all - check your alarm's instructions. We've got a (brown) bonnet pin switch wire which can stay in the engine bay. The rest? Get out the electrical tape (or plastic spiral), and wrap that bunch of wires into a neat loom, to go inside.

07 We're getting quite good at feeding wires into our Punto (look in the auxiliary fusebox section for our chosen method - all we've done is enlarged the hole we made in the grommet). Any wiring holes you drill yourself must be fitted with a grommet if you want the alarm to be reliable.

As long as the battery stays off, you might as well plug in the loom to the back of the module now. After that, the module can be fitted to its bracket, but make sure you can still get to the sensitivity adjuster.

The bonnet pin switch should be close to the battery, but it must hit a 'good' (flat) spot on the bonnet - getting this right can be tricky. The Punto has an ideal spot on the slam panel behind the headlight. Stick on a few strips of masking tape first - this gives you something to mark on . . .

. . . and it stops the drill slipping. We need two holes - one large, for the switch body, and a smaller one for the switch retaining screw.

Crimp on a small spade connector to the pin switch wire, connect up to the pin switch, then slip the whole thing into the hole you just made . . .

08

09

10

11

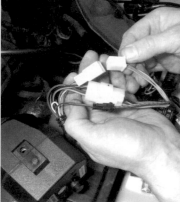

>>

Tricks 'n' tips

You can test your bonnet pin switch with a simple test light, connected between the pin switch spade connection and the battery positive (+) terminal. With the bonnet shut, the light should be out - as soon as it's opened on the catch, the light should be on. Trimming the pin switch down will make it come on sooner, but only take off a little plastic at a time, then re-test.

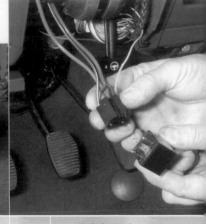

>>

12 . . . and tighten the screw securely - this is the switch's earth connection to the car body, so it has to be tight.

13 Back inside the car, it's time for some serious wiring-up. Let's do the immobiliser relay first. Undo the Allen screws under the steering column, and remove the lower shroud for access to the ignition switch wiring. Cut the red wire on the plug, and bare the two ends. Join the brown and red/white wires from the relay socket to the plug-end red wire . . .

14 . . . and the other brown to the red wire going off into the wiring loom. Solid, well-insulated connections needed here. Now plug in the relay to the socket, and that's the immobiliser done. Tape or cable-tie the relay in place under the dash.

19 . . . and the alarm wiring can be fed through behind, right up to the fusebox's doorstep. Though it takes a little more work, this approach is better than feeding wiring over the pedals, where it might drop down at an inconvenient moment...

20 Let's go back to that LED, before we forget. Our Punto has a handy blank switch in the centre of the dash, ideal for slipping an LED into - remember, for max effect, this needs to be somewhere highly-visible from outside. To get to this switch, undo the two screws at the top of the centre panel . . .

21 . . . then remove the stereo (see the ICE section) and remove the two screws below the heater control panel.

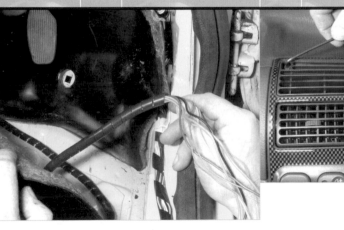

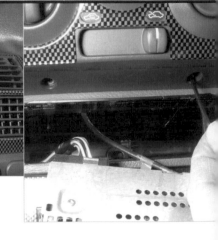

15 Feed the alarm wiring across the car, looming it up as you go. Here, we've separated out the alarm LED and its wire, which is going to the centre part of the dash. It's called forward planning.

16 To make a neat job of running the wiring across to the fusebox (on the driver's side), the carpet's got to come up. Which means removing the clutch foot rest (three screws, wash your hands afterwards) . . .

17 . . . and unclip the carpet from the dash/centre console.

18 Now remove the clips securing the sound-deadening . . .

22 Pull off the fan control knob, and remove the screw behind it . . .

23 . . . then ease the heater control panel off the dash.

24 Just two more screws to go now, below the switch panel . . .

25 . . . and out it comes. Remove the switch wiring plug at the rear of the panel, and it's at your mercy.

>>

>>

26 Holy smokes - not more screws! This time it's the switch illumination panel we're taking off . . .

27 . . . before finally, we can prise out that blank switch. This should be a sweet-looking result, but we've had to work for this!

28 Drill a hole in the switch blank (typically, it's an 8 mm hole for an LED holder) . . .

Like our Haynes manual wiring diagram said, it was a light blue (RH) and light blue/black (LH) pair of wires we wanted. Join one alarm grey wire to each Fiat original, and we're sorted. Note we stripped a little insulation off the original wires, wrapped the new ones around, then used solder.

32 Makes a permanent, reliable connection - tape it up afterwards.

We took the same approach, wiring-in the central locking function. Our Haynes diagram showed us the lock wire should be white, and the unlock wire light blue. On went the blue and green alarm wires, and hey presto - remote locking, allowing us to de-lock the doors later on. Sweet.

33

To give triggering on the interior light, our alarm's red wire has to go straight to the interior light circuit. Now we want a red/white Fiat wire, but there's several to choose from round the fusebox. Go for the one nearest the fuse itself, and you'll be alright. Remember, all these soldered joints get well-insulated with tape when we're done.

34

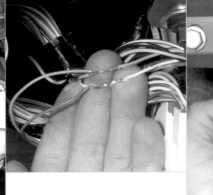

29 . . . then the switch panel can be rebuilt and refitted, leaving the LED poking through.

30 Now fit the LED into its holder, and push the holder back into the drilled switch. The modified switch can now be clipped back to the panel. Simple, eh? Not.

31 Well, fitting the LED was a bit of a pig, but rest easy - the remaining jobs are pretty simple. Let's get the indicators in-sync with the alarm first. Tracing the indicator wires at the fusebox is easy-peas with a test light (temporarily reconnect the battery, and switch them on).

So come on - does it work? Most alarms require you to 'programme in' the remotes before they'll work. Test all the alarm features in turn, remembering to allow enough time for the alarm to arm itself (usually about 30 seconds). When you test it for the first time, either shut the bonnet completely, or do like us, and hold the bonnet pin switch down. Our way, you can pull out the alarm fuses and shut it up, if something goes wrong!

Set the anti-shock sensitivity with a thought to where you live and park - will it be set off every night by the neighbour's cat, or by kids playing football? Finally, and most important of all - next time you park up, remember to set it!

35 Last, there's a yellow wire which connects to the yellow on our immobiliser relay . . .

36 . . . and a black wire, which goes to a good earth point. Fiat thoughtfully provide one, right below the car's fusebox - just remove the bolt, add your ring-terminalled wire, and tighten back up. That's it!

37

38

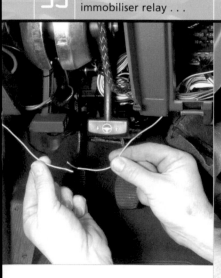
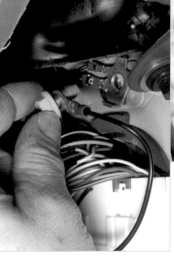
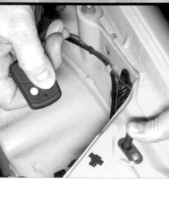

Body styling

If you're planning a major body job, you've probably already got some good ideas about how you want your Punto to look, from *'Max Power'* or *'Revs'*, or maybe from a friend's car. While it can be good to have a target car to aim for, if you're just starting out on the road towards a fully-loaded car, you probably don't want (or can't quite afford) to go 'all the way' all at once.

If you're new to the world of modifying, it's a good idea to start with smaller jobs, and work up to the full body kit gradually, as your skills increase; spending loads on a body kit is a pretty lame idea if you then make a mess of fitting it! There's plenty of small ways to improve the look of your Punto, which don't cost much, and which are simple enough to fit; start with some of these before you go too mad!

One golden rule with any body mods is to plan what you're going to do, and don't rush it. It's better that the car looks a bit stupid for a week (because you couldn't get something finished) than to rush a job and have the car look stupid forever. Do half the job properly instead of messing up all of it. Try and think the jobs through - plan each stage. Have you got all the tools, screws or whatever before you start, or will you have to break off halfway through? If you get stuck, is there someone you can get to help, or have they gone off for the weekend? Above all, if something goes wrong - don't panic - a calm approach will prove to be a huge bonus (that job doesn't have to be done today, does it?).

If a piece of trim won't come off, don't force it. If something feels like it's going to break, it probably will - stop and consider whether to go on and break it, or try another approach. You could even try the Haynes manual… Especially on an older car, things either never come off as easily as you think, or else have already been off so many times that they break or won't fit back on properly. While we'd all like to do a perfect job every time, working on an older car will, sooner or later, teach you the fine art of 'bodging' (finding valid alternative ways of fixing things!). Don't assume you'll have to bodge something back on, every time - if a trim clip breaks when you take something off, it might be easier and cheaper than you think to simply go to your Fiat dealer, and buy a new clip (remember, even Fiat mechanics break things from time to time, so they will keep these things in stock!).

Mirror, mirror

Mirrors are another simple to fit, must-have accessory. The DTM or M3-style door mirrors are well established on the modified car circuit, but there are lots of variations of mirror styles and finishes, so finding some you like won't be hard.

If you want to be just a little different, try some 'California' mirrors. The trouble with being different is it's always more work - California mirrors are 'universal fit', meaning you have to make them fit your car. You bought a Punto 'cause it's a popular car, so why make life difficult? Buy some Punto mirrors (or at least some Punto mirror bases), and your new mirrors could be fitted in minutes.

There's more to mirrors than just looks, though - some have toys attached. Like side repeater lights (in a Merc stylee) or thumb switches for releasing your de-locked, de-handled doors. We want some of that.

DTM cup **mirrors**

01 Your first task is to remove that nasty standard mirror assembly. What you do with said mirror is up to you, but we would advise keeping them safe – you never know when you might need a replacement! Start by opening the door, and locate the rubber cover on the adjustment lever. Prise this cover off.

02 Next, using a suitable tool (circlip pliers work great here, if you have some), unscrew and remove the locking collar from the adjustment lever.

03 Prise away the plastic trim panel . . .

04 . . . to reveal the three mirror securing screws.

05 Remove the screws, supporting the mirror with one hand - even if you're going to chuck it, you'd be a bit gutted if your old mirror damaged the bodywork on its way to the floor.

06 They're not the nastiest standard mirrors ever, but they're still standard.

07 We're going to fit DTM cup style mirrors to our car – they're purposely designed for the Punto which makes fitment easy. Try and ignore universal fitment mirrors; as the name suggests, they can fit any car – but not very well, without a lot of work. The first job now is to secure the mirror mounting plate to the actual mirror, with the three screws supplied with the kit.

08 Pop the mirror assembly into place on the car, and supporting the unit with one hand, secure it in place using the three screws and washers supplied with the kit. Not much effort there, then.

09 Hide the evidence by refitting the inner plastic trim panel.

10 Our new mirrors don't have levers for internal adjustment (the mirror glass is tilted by hand), which leaves us with a hole to plug. A neat way of doing this is to buy a rubber grommet (any DIY store or car accessory shop should sell these) and plug the hole in the trim panel. That's it - time for a beer.

Water features

This is all about giving you a couple of highly-visible features up front. Forget Charlie Dimmock. Do not even think Charlie Dimmock. Washer jet lights are now almost expected at a cruise, and it's such a simple feature to fit, it's nearly a crime not to. Course, our friendly fellas in blue uniforms don't see it quite that way - showing anything other than a white light up front is illegal, and plenty of people get stopped for it. The best answer? Fit them by all means, but rig them into a well-placed switch for emergencies.

01 Removing the boring standard washer jets is easy, and will take no time at all. On the underside of the bonnet, pull off the pipe that leads from the washer bottle to the jets (start it moving by prising the end of the pipe with a wee screwdriver).

02 Then remove the existing washer jets by pressing the retaining lugs in, and lifting the jet out. Try not to break them - you might be refitting them one day.

03 Here's all the bits you're likely to be faced with, laid out in the right fitting order. Notice the thick plastic washer has a slot cut in it - this is supposed to be for the wire from the new jet to pass through (they think of everything, don't they?).

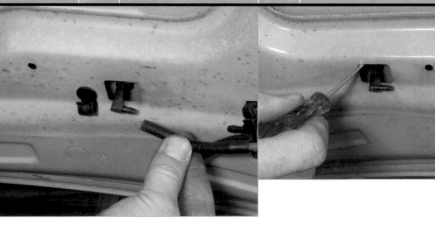

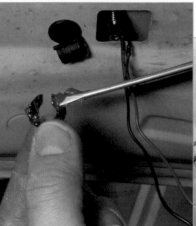

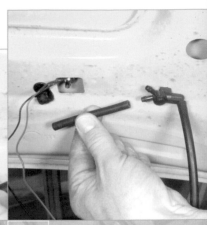

04 Fitting the new washer in the bonnet hole's the easy part. Fitting all the washers and the nut into the tiny little hole underneath - well, that's a little trickier. We used grease to 'stick' the first plastic washer (the one with the slot) in place . . .

05 . . . and if you put enough on, the next two washers (flat and split type) will also stick well enough, at least for a second . . .

06 . . . while you grab the nut in some tweezers, and get it started on the thread. Bit fiddly, this job.

07 Now the jets are sitting proudly on our bonnet, it's time to connect them up - to water, and to electric. The water side of things gave us our first real problem - the original washer tube is too short.

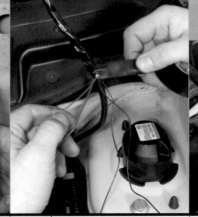

08 Fortunately, you can buy washer tubing in most car accessory shops. Cut it to length (be a bit generous, but don't let the tube bunch up, or the water won't flow), warm up the end to make it flexible, and push firmly onto the pipe stubs.

09 To make a neat job of running the wiring down into the engine bay, tape it to the washer tubing. This is a whole lot better than having the wires just hanging from the jets, where they could drop down onto the engine, and melt.

10 The two red wires are obviously the lives, and we're going to run these from the live supply to the front sidelights. To make the wiring a bit easier, we stripped and joined our two red wires to another (single) red, which will run to the back of the headlights. You could use bullets for this, but we like our soldering iron too much.

11 Down at the headlight wiring plug, whip out your test light. With the sidelights switched on, you're looking for the only wire that's live (in our case, it was yellow/black).

>>

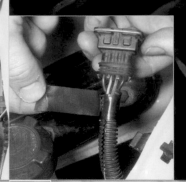

12 Our mechanic's performing surgery on our Fiat wiring with a scalpel, and he's not even a proper doctor! Stripping off a little yellow/black insulation like this gives us a way of tapping into the car's original wiring, without cutting it.

13 Introduce our red wire from the washer jets, wrap it round the bare bit of sidelight-live wire . . .

14 . . . then solder to make a good joint . . .

15 . . . and insulate the finished job for safety. That's a solid, reliable connection we've just made.

If you're happy just to have your washer jet lights working off your sidelights, join the two black wires from the jets together, and run them to an earth point under the bonnet (the battery negative terminal would do). We wanted our jets on a switch, so having joined our two blacks into one wire, we fed it through using the same grommet we'd used for our ICE install.

Discreet little switch under the dash, or major interior feature? Can't make much of a few switches, can you? Oh, but we can. Here's what we've got planned for the very un-interesting tray below the stereo - our own custom-made switch panel, which will also house a switch for interior neons and a starter button.

This is an alloy bit of plate we've cut to size, and covered with masking tape (which protects the finish, and makes it easy to mark out). With the positions for our three switches marked, drill them out as big as you can . . .

. . . and finish off with a file.

16

17

18

19

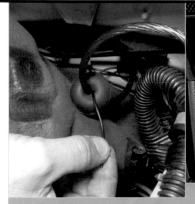

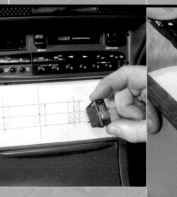

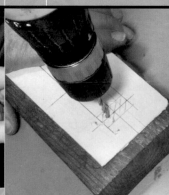

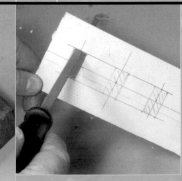

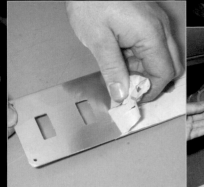

20 Peel off the masking tape, and it's a very trick-looking panel already. Our Punto's interior theme is yellow and black, so it won't come as a huge surprise that we covered our panel in carbon-fibre film (see 'Interiors').

21 Enough fabrication - back to the wiring. Feed the black wire (from the engine bay) through to the centre console . . .

22 . . . then into the back of the new panel, and join it to one switch terminal with a spade connector. In case you were wondering, the switches we used slip through the holes in our panel, and clip into place from behind.

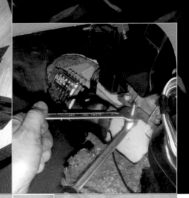

23 All we need now is an earth point. With the carpet pulled down in front of the centre console, we made our own by drilling a hole and fitting a bolt up through from below (if this seems a bit much to you, drill a smaller hole and use a self-tapper).

24 Slip a ring terminal onto another piece of black wire, attach it to earth . . .

25 . . . and make it secure. If you've chosen an earth point where the metal's painted, scrape the paint away to make a clean connection.

26 And here's one switch panel we covered earlier. Drill four neat holes in the corners, and secure with four (black) self-tappers. Sweet-as.

Smoothly does it

If you've bought a basic Punto, it's understandable that you might not want to declare this fact loudly from the rear end of your car. Badges also clutter up the otherwise clean lines, and besides, you're trying to make your Punto look different, so why give them obvious clues like a badge? Most Puntos also come with admittedly-useful but actually quite ugly side rubbing strips of some sort - lose these, or at least colour-code, if you're at all serious about raising your game.

De-badging

01 The Fiat badge on the front is bolted on, so removing that is no challenge - open the bonnet and unbolt it from behind. Virtually all the other badges they use just peel off. Soften the glue up with a heatgun first . . .

02 . . . then start prising them off. Either use a plastic tool like this, or put some card behind your favourite screwdriver, to save the paintwork.

03 Clean off the gluey remains with some solvent, and you're a step closer to cleaning up your bodywork.

De-stripping

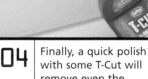

01 Side rubbing strips. Good - they save your paint if Mr Numpty opens his rusty Metro door into your car. Bad - they look hideous. If looks are important, removal is an option (as is colour-coding, if you want to keep them). Warm them up like your badges, then start peeling them off at one end.

02 The gluey residue left on the bodywork needs to be cleaned off - brake cleaner is ace for doing this.

03 Alternatively, if you have the real thing (a drill-mounted pinstripe removing tool, being modelled here by our mechanic) use that!

04 Finally, a quick polish with some T-Cut will remove even the toughest dirt, and blend-in the paint behind the strip nicely.

01 When it comes to car bodywork, every hole is not a goal. At least small holes can be filled without stretching your talent envelope too far. First, cover the area around your chosen hole (two holes, in this case) with masking tape - make sure you get a decent working area around the hole.

Filling holes - a cunning plan

02 Now neatly cut out your holes in the tape.

03 Here's where we start to see the true cunning of this plan - mix up some Araldite (or similar glue for bonding metals), and apply a blob of it to a washer large enough to cover the hole, on the inside. Rich types among you may prefer to use a coin.

04 Stick the washer or coin on from inside, then stand around looking stupid, holding it in place while the glue dries.

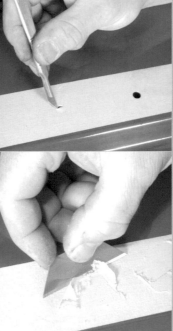
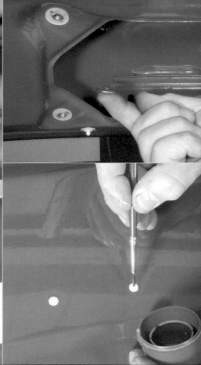

05 Mix up some filler, and apply to your hole - the masking tape prevents any getting on the paintwork. Apply more than one layer, and build the filler up evenly.

06 We found that the filler could be trimmed flat using a sharp Stanley blade, used at a very shallow angle. The filler doesn't really 'take' to the masking tape, making it easier to trim away the excess.

07 Peel away the masking tape, and your hole is filled - all it needs is paint.

08 If you haven't done such a great job, remember that you can improve things by applying layer after layer of paint (wait for each one to dry). When you've built the paint up proud of the hole, T-Cut it back smooth.

Tailgate/boot lid
smoothing

Achieving the 'fully-flushed' look isn't too involved a procedure, providing you know someone who can weld, and is handy with filler and spray. Completely smoothing the back end is a logical extension of de-badging - the first thing to go is the tailgate rear wiper. Rear wipers are undoubtedly useful, and were put there for a good reason, but hey - that's just boring.

If you're going to de-lock the tailgate, some means of opening the thing afterwards would be handy, if only so your mates can admire your ICE install. You'll be needing a boot release solenoid, then - not too hard to wire one up. All you've got to do is fill the large hole left by removing the lock barrel, and it's too big for filler alone.

Also too big for just filler is the number plate recess. And where's that number plate going, and how will it be lit up at night? And you thought dealing with gaping holes in your tailgate was hard. Well, don't worry - your friends at Haynes are on the case for you now...

Rear wiper **removal**

01 Flip up the plastic cap on your rear wiper, and undo the nut. Pretty simple so far.

02 Prising the wiper arm off its spindle is where things can get sticky - some almost fall off, while others need persuasion. If you're levering with a large screwdriver, use some folded-up card to protect the paintwork.

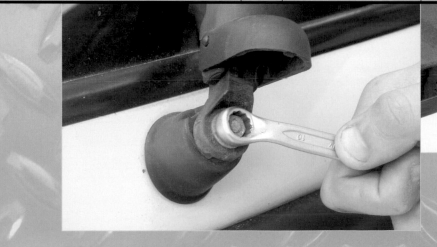

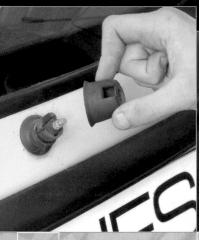

03 Last job 'outside' is removing the plastic trim cap surrounding the wiper spindle and the washer jet.

04 The trim panel inside the tailgate is next to go, and it's secured by a few screws . . .

05 . . . and plastic clips round the edge, which you just prise free.

06 Before unbolting the wiper motor, pull the washer supply hose off the pipe stub . . .

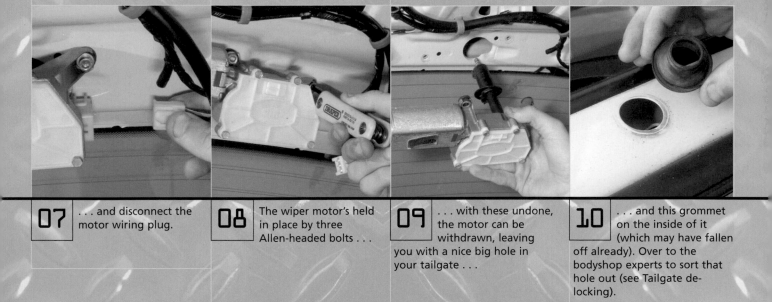

07 . . . and disconnect the motor wiring plug.

08 The wiper motor's held in place by three Allen-headed bolts . . .

09 . . . with these undone, the motor can be withdrawn, leaving you with a nice big hole in your tailgate . . .

10 . . . and this grommet on the inside of it (which may have fallen off already). Over to the bodyshop experts to sort that hole out (see Tailgate de-locking).

Tailgate **de-locking**

01 For a complete boot-smooth, the tailgate lock has to go as well. Unbolt the tailgate catch (this will have to go back on later, or you'll have a bit of a problem keeping the boot shut) . . .

02 . . . and withdraw it (there's another grommet fitted to this item, too, but you've seen enough already).

03 Unclip the plastic cover from the back of the catch . . .

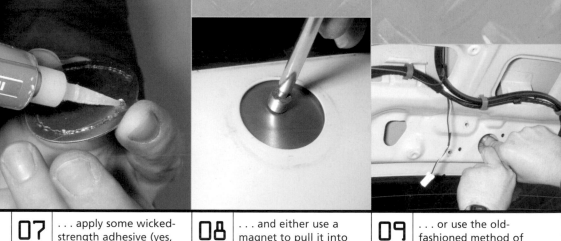

07 . . . apply some wicked-strength adhesive (yes, really) . . .

08 . . . and either use a magnet to pull it into place . . .

09 . . . or use the old-fashioned method of pressing it in from behind.

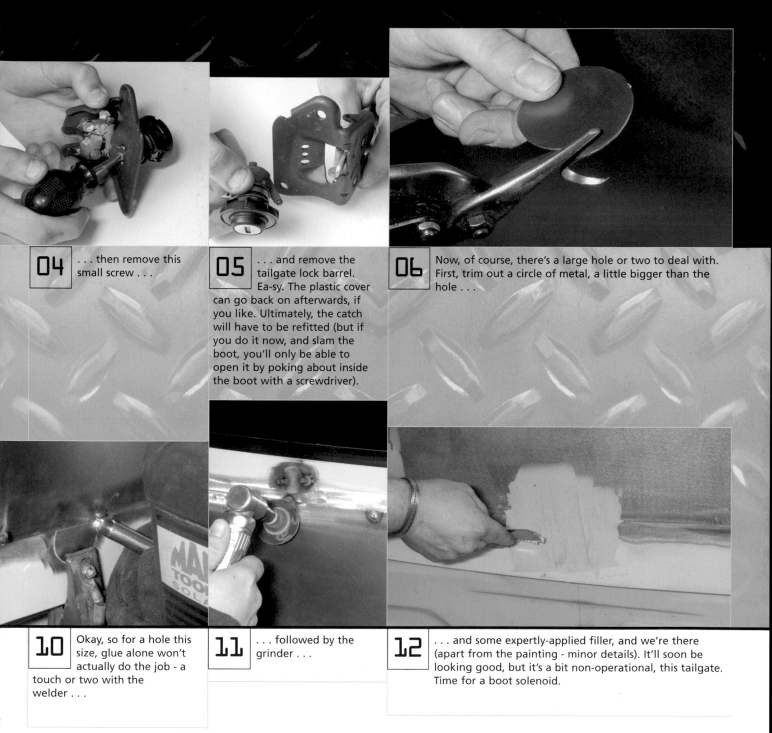

04 . . . then remove this small screw . . .

05 . . . and remove the tailgate lock barrel. Ea-sy. The plastic cover can go back on afterwards, if you like. Ultimately, the catch will have to be refitted (but if you do it now, and slam the boot, you'll only be able to open it by poking about inside the boot with a screwdriver).

06 Now, of course, there's a large hole or two to deal with. First, trim out a circle of metal, a little bigger than the hole . . .

10 Okay, so for a hole this size, glue alone won't actually do the job - a touch or two with the welder . . .

11 . . . followed by the grinder . . .

12 . . . and some expertly-applied filler, and we're there (apart from the painting - minor details). It'll soon be looking good, but it's a bit non-operational, this tailgate. Time for a boot solenoid.

Tailgate **solenoid**

 01 We've chosen to mount our switch on the trim panel that hides the main fusebox (two screws). A hole drilled in the trim, and the switch is ready to be popped into place. We're using a clever spring-loaded switch that springs back once depressed (no worries about turning switches off, or leaving them on).

02 Two lengths of wire needed here (we've chosen some stylish purple wire for this install). One goes off to a live feed, which you could source at the battery or fusebox (we're taking ours from our own fusebox - see 'security'). The other wire will need to run to the tailgate, so make sure you've got plenty.

03 With the switch fitted, the trim panel can go back on. The switch is nicely concealed and is unlikely to be knocked accidentally, reducing the possibility of your boot popping open.

04 The wire can then be routed down to the tailgate. Run the wire along the door sills, under the carpet and seats into the boot and up the C-pillar. Try and do it so the wire's not visible (especially if it's purple!).

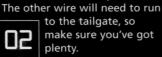

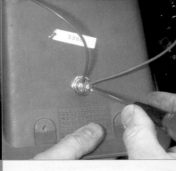

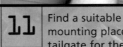

09 The next part requires a length of 6 mm threaded rod (DIY store). Because you can't mount the solenoid in line with the boot catch, a lever has to be fitted to the lock catch, to drop down to the level of the solenoid - this is it. Fit the bar to the hole you drilled in the catch with a screw.

10 With the second hole drilled at the other end of the bar, fit the lock assembly back into place.

11 Find a suitable mounting place on the tailgate for the central locking solenoid, mark and drill the 2 holes required. Once you've decided on a good place, thread the solenoid plunger through the hole in the bar . . .

12 . . . then tighten the retaining screws. You'll have noticed we've used one of the screw holes as an earth point for the solenoid (blue wire). The solenoid live feed's green; there are three other wires (black, brown and white) which you don't need, so tape them up and forget about them.

05 When you have the wire as far as possible up the C-pillar (i.e. to the roof), remove the rubber seal that holds the roof lining in place, and allow it to drop down slightly. You can then feed the wire under the roof lining and on to the tailgate by passing it up through the hole where the main wiring loom is situated.

06 This is the tricky part. You now have to route the wire down to bottom half of the tailgate. The only way you can do this is by attaching the end to a length of welding wire and poking it down the side channels of the tailgate, until you come out at the bottom.

07 The wire can then be fed along the tailgate, held in place by threading it through the existing cable-ties.

08 Now you need to start doctoring parts. Firstly remove the tailgate catch assembly, held in place by two screws. Take a file to the catch to remove the case-hardening (brass-coloured top coating), then drill a small hole in the catch.

13 The green wire from the solenoid is then joined to the wire routed up from the switch.

14 To keep everything in its right place, screw a cable nipple onto the plunger rod, behind where the threaded bar naturally rests. You can get these cable nipples from bike shops and some car accessory places.

15 Your final job is to fit a spring to the plunger rod, so that when the catch is released, the rod and bar move back into the correct position again. Drill a tiny hole in the inner skin of the tailgate and attach one end of the spring to that hole. Then simply attach the spring to the cable nipple and you're finished. One working home-made solenoid kit - nice.

16 Just one more job! When we tried to refit the tailgate trim panel, the handle recess in it was hitting our new solenoid. But the trim panel's plastic, and we've got lots of sharp tools to play with. Game over.

Tailgate **smoothing**

Body styling

01 Once you've de-wipered and de-locked the cluttered Punto rear end, what's left? The trim strip above the number plate, that's what. Luckily, removal is pretty easy - the trim's held in place with two Allen bolts . . .

02 . . . then remember to disconnect the number plate light wiring plug inside the tailgate, before lifting the trim strip away.

03 The best way of flushing a tailgate is to weld a metal plate over the number plate recess. So a template of the recess must be made - paper or card are good materials to use for this.

04 The paper template can then be transferred to metal, and the plate is ready.

05 Offer the metal plate into position to check that it's exactly the right shape. Now we're using a special tool to punch holes around the edge of the metal (you could always use a drill) - you'll see why we've made these holes later.

06 In order for the welder to do its job properly, the paint around the edge of the recess must be taken back to bare metal using an angle-grinder.

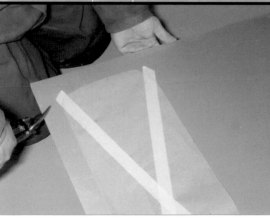

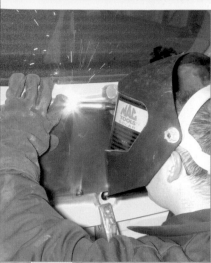

07 It's time to start welding the plate into place, by welding up each of the holes we created earlier (only use the welder in short bursts, or excess heat may distort the tailgate). Welding the plate this way means you don't run the risk of totally grinding the weld out later, and it doesn't give you yet another edge to try and smooth in.

08 Halfway through the welding process, it may be necessary to use a tool such as ball-peen (rounded-end) hammer to encourage the edge of the plate to stay in place, as it will naturally move when heat from the welder passes over it.

09 Once the welding is finished, the excess can be removed using the faithful grinder.

10 Last but not least, it's filler time! Use the least amount of filler you can, 'cause you don't want to risk that filler shrinking in time and forcing you to have the job done again. Once the filler is completely dried, it's ready for sanding, priming and painting.

Number plate mounting and lighting

If your rear bumper has no provision for a number plate (and there's plenty out there without this rather essential feature), contact Venom Motorsport, who produce a quality ready-made number plate recess in fibreglass. Bonus. All you do then is offer it up, and mark the **01** bumper for cutting it in.

This rear bumper didn't give much scope for plate mounting, so we made two little brackets, and slung it underneath. Fortunately, it still shows up well enough not to **02** attract the flashing-blue-light kind of attention.

This lighting solution might not be strictly legal, but at least we tried, and again, this might be enough of a gesture to avoid getting pulled. A row of white LEDs mounted above the plate will hopefully be bright enough to do the job. Wired, in case you wondered, **03** from the existing number plate light circuit.

Though you probably wouldn't think it, this is one of the most forgotten-about items - and it causes no end of problems. Try and think ahead when planning a boot-smooth, as an illegal number plate is a bit of a come-and-nick-me to you-know-who.

Single wiper
conversion

Another saloon-car racing-inspired item, the single wiper conversion is a really smart way to make your Punto stand out from the crowd.

Presumably, the saloon racers fit single wipers to enhance the view forward (one less wiper arm obscuring the view could make all the difference), improve the aerodynamics, and maybe even to save weight! Many Punto owners want the single wiper because it helps to remove clutter - park two Puntos side by side, and the one with one less wiper looks way better. It's a fairly 'neutral' mod, too - unlike some, it works as well on a 'sport-Punto' as on a 'luxury-Punto'.

01 First things to go are your old wipers (well, no surprise there, then). Make sure the wipers are 'parked' by switching them on, then quickly off, then let the wipers come to rest before switching off the ignition. Prise up the nut cover on each wiper arm . . .

02 . . . and undo the 13 mm nut underneath. After that, your old wipers can be prised off their splines and removed.

03 With the wipers gone, the next item to remove is the windscreen scuttle panel, which is held on by a total of eight screws (don't lose 'em).

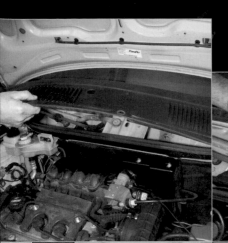

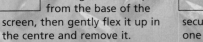

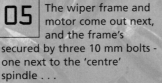

> 04 Pull the panel towards the engine to unclip it from the base of the screen, then gently flex it up in the centre and remove it.

05 The wiper frame and motor come out next, and the frame's secured by three 10 mm bolts - one next to the 'centre' spindle . . .

06 . . . one next to the 'outer' spindle . . .

07 . . . and the last one in front of the wiper motor itself.

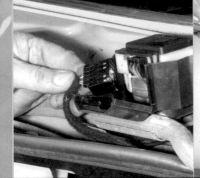

08 Lift the wiper frame up (bearing in mind the wiper motor wiring's still connected), and turn it over. Open the plastic cover on the motor, then disconnect the wiring plug by squeezing the clip. Unclip the wiring from the frame, then remove the frame from the car, and take it to a clean working area (the pavement next to your Punto is not what we had in mind).

09 Time for a little dismantling of your linkage, and time for you to get acquainted with the wiper motor arm, which is about 50 mm long, splined onto the wiper motor shaft, and attached to it by a single nut. Undo this nut without turning the wiper motor arm, by holding the square end of the arm in one open-end spanner . . .

10 . . . then prise the motor arm off the motor spindle, again without turning it.

11 Now the spindles both have to be removed from the wiper frame. Removing the circlips which hold the spindles in isn't hard. Finding them afterwards, when they've flown off into space, is trickier. Luckily, you shouldn't need them again - new circlips are supplied.

>>

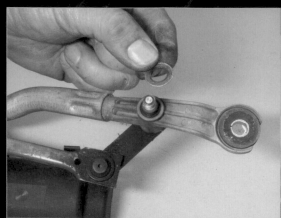

>>

12 After the circlip, there's a plain washer to remove . . .

13 . . . and a rubber O-ring - we'll be re-using these two bits in a minute, so don't lose them.

14 The spindles should just slide out of the wiper frame, but sometimes, life's just not that simple. Recover the washer from the base of the old spindle - we'll be recycling that. When you're finished, you should have a pretty bare-looking wiper frame with a motor attached.

19 . . . then on goes the other old washer we took off after the original circlip was removed . . .

20 . . . and finally, it all gets pinned together using one of the new circlips provided - make sure it enters the groove in the new spindle properly, and snaps home.

21 Fit the new motor arm onto the motor splines, so that the arm lies directly under the linkage, like this. Using the same trick as before (one spanner to hold the square end of the arm, and another to do the tightening), fit and tighten the motor arm nut. Again, don't turn the motor shaft while doing this.

15 And here's the new single-wiper-sized linkage (you can tell it's the new one - it's a whole lot shinier). First, it's on with the washer we just removed from the base of the old wiper spindle . . .

16 . . . then add a generous dollop of grease . . .

17 . . . and slip it into the old frame. Fitting a single wiper kit is very much like making love to a beautiful woman...

18 Next, there's the old rubber O-ring to fit (this seals in all that grease) . . .

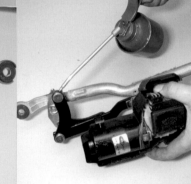

22 Before you go ahead and fit the new linkage, check that it looks like ours. In particular, the motor arm should lie directly under the main link arm, and at the other end, the curved sections of linkage should cross over in an X pattern.

23 It's worth giving the linkage pivots a drop or two of lube before fitting.

24 Offer the new linkage into place on the car, plug the wiper motor back in, then refit the motor plastic cover.

25 The frame can now be bolted back in, same as before, with the three 10 mm bolts. Check there's no stray wiring around the linkage, which might get caught up in there. Before fitting the wiper arm, switch on the ignition, and flick the wiper on, then off (let them 'park'). Check that the wiper motor arm still lies directly under the link arm, as before.

>>

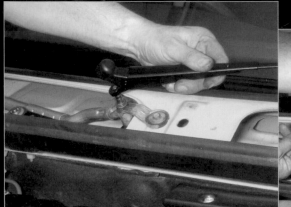

>>

26 Fit the new wiper arm, and secure it with the nut provided. To start with, fit the wiper to park on the left - this is the default position. And do not be tempted to put the wipers on just yet, either.

27 Work the new linkage by hand, and see how the wiper moves. What we're trying to do first is to set the wiper blade's sweep - ie we're trying to get it to go equally across both sides of the screen.

28 Re-position the wiper arm on the spindle until it's just right, and tighten the arm nut securely. That part is now done, and the wiper arm is set.

29 Next, we set the parked position of the motor, by undoing the motor arm nut and re-positioning the motor arm on its spindle. This can only be done by try-it-and-see. For centre parking, set the motor arm vertical, like this - if you want it off to one side, leave it horizontal.

30 The last job is refitting the scuttle panel, which we've left off while making our adjustments. Refitting the panel means the wiper's got to come off again, so to avoid losing its carefully-found setting, mark the blade's position on the screen with a strip of masking tape.

31 The final act of consigning your unwanted extra wiper to the bin is to fit the blanking grommet over the driver's side spindle hole. Phew - that's it. Time for a well-earned pint.

Travelling **incognito**

If you is a gangsta wiv da Staines massive, blacking those windows is a must. Window tinting is also one of the best ways to disguise a naff standard interior, or a good way to hide a sorted interior (or ICE install) from the crims...

Tints look right with almost any car colour (limo-tint on a black Punto is virtually essential, while mirror film looks trick on a silver car), and with 'reflex film' available in various rainbow colours, there's something for everyone. Only downside is - not all tints are legal to be run on the road, and you'll be chancing it buying any advertised as 'for show cars only'. The boys in blue don't like to see tinted front windows (at cruises, it can be an instant pull), but just doing the rear windows looks a bit stupid. Tints don't suit everybody - if you're doing your car to pose around in (and why not?) it's hard enough to see you in there anyway, without blacking-out the windows!

Because window tinting involves sticking a layer of film to the inside of the glass, fitting tints might help to prevent a break-in, since your side windows won't shatter when hit. Car security firm Toad market an adhesive film specifically designed to prevent break-ins in this way, and even humble window-tinting kits are claimed to offer the same effect.

Generally, window tint comes on a roll, but you can sometimes buy pre-cut kits for popular cars. Buying a kit (if you can) sounds a better deal, but if you muck up fitting one section, you'll be buying another complete kit. With a roll of film, check how many windows you'll be able to do with it - one roll usually isn't enough for the whole car.

At this point, we'd better 'fess up and tell you that tinting will severely try your patience. If you're not a patient sort of person, this is one job which may well wind you up - you have been warned. Saying that, if you're calm and careful, and you follow the instructions to the letter, you could surprise yourself - our mechanic did, when we tried it for the first time and got a near-perfect result!

In brief, the process for tinting is to lay the film on the outside of the glass first, and cut it exactly to size. The protective layer is peeled off to expose the adhesive side, the film is transferred to the inside of the car (tricky) and then squeegeed into place (also tricky). All this must be done with scrupulous cleanliness, as any muck or stray bits of trimmed-off film will ruin the effect (tricky, if you're working outside). The other problem which won't surprise you is that getting rid of air bubbles and creases can take time. A long time. This is another test of patience, because if, as the instructions say, you've used plenty of spray, it will take a while to dry out and stick... just don't panic!

Legal eagle

The law on window tinting currently is that there must be no more than a 25% reduction in light transmission through windscreens, and a limit of 30% reduction on all other glass. How the heck do you measure light reduction? Also, many cars come with tinted glass as standard - so can you fit a tinting kit on top and still be legal? Hard to know what line to take, if you're stopped by Plod - try and choose a tinting kit which is EC-approved (ask before you buy, and if you think it could be a serious issue, get a letter from the company to support the legality of the kit, to use in your defence). Some forces now take this seriously enough to have portable test equipment they can use at the roadside - if your car fails, it's an on-the-spot fine.

Tinting windows

It's worth picking your day, and your working area, pretty carefully - on a windy day, there'll be more dust in the air, and it'll be a nightmare trying to stop the film flapping and folding onto itself while you're working.

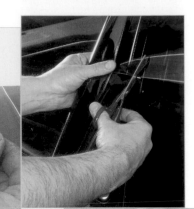

Applying window tint is best done on a warm day (or in a warm garage - if there is such a thing), because the adhesive will begin to dry sooner. For fairly obvious reasons, don't try tinting when it's starting to get dark! It's a good idea to have a mate to help out with this job, but you might get fed up hearing 'you've missed another bubble' or 'you can still see that crease, y'know'.

01 Get the window being tinted clean - really clean - inside and out. Don't use glass cleaners (or any other product) containing ammonia or vinegar, since both will react with the film or its adhesive, and muck it up. Also clean the area around the window - it's too easy for stray dirt to attach itself to the film - and by the time you've noticed it, it could be too late. On door windows, wind them down slightly, to clean all of the top edge, then close them tight to fit the film.

02 Before you even unroll the film, take note - handle it carefully. If you crease it, you won't get the creases out - ever. First work out which way up the film is, by applying a small bit of really sticky tape to the front and back side - use the tape to pull the films apart, just at one corner.

03 Lay the film onto the glass, with the clear side facing you. Unroll the film, and cut it roughly to the size of the window (on a door window, leave plenty at the bottom edge for now). Some kits have a logo on the film, which seems daft - tinting's difficult enough, without having to get a logo straight! The only benefit of a logo is to establish which layer is the tint. Make life easier - lose the logo.

04 Spray the outside of the window with a weak soapy water solution (Folia Tec supply a small bottle of Joy fluid in their kit, but you could use a few drops of ordinary washing-up liquid). Get one of those plant sprayers you can buy cheap in any DIY store, if your kit doesn't contain a sprayer.

05 Lay the roughly-cut sheet of tint back onto the glass, and spray the outside of the film with soapy water . . .

06 . . . then use a squeegee to get out the air bubbles, sticking the film to the outside of the glass.

07 On a door window, trim the bottom edge to leave some excess to tuck down inside the door - this stops the film peeling off on the bottom rubber when you roll the window down!

08 Using a sharp knife (and taking care not to damage your paint or the window rubber), trim round the outside of the window. A piece of plastic (like an expired video club card) is brilliant for tucking the film into the edges to get the shape right, but don't trim the film right to the absolute edge - leave a small, even gap of just a few mill all round (this helps to get rid of excess water when you squeegee it on the inside - you'll see).

09 Now go inside, and prepare for receiving the tint. On fixed glass, waterproof the side trim panels in anticipation of the soapy water which will be used, by taping on some plastic sheet (otherwise, you'll have some very soggy panels. And seats. And carpets). Spray the inside of the glass with the soapy solution.

10 Back outside, it's time to separate the films. Use two pieces of sticky tape to pull the films slightly apart at one corner. As the films come apart, spray more solution onto the tinted piece underneath, to help it separate cleanly. Try not to lift the tint film too much off the glass when separating, as this increases the risk of creasing.

11 Have your willing helper on standby, to assist with transferring the film to the inside (a prime time for messing it all up). Peel the tint film off the glass, keeping it as flat as you can. Without letting it fold onto itself, move it inside the car and place it fairly accurately on the inside of the glass. The surface which was outside should now be on the inside of the glass (now that you've cut it, it will only fit one way!). Carefully slide the film into the corners, keeping it flat.

12 On a door window, use your plastic to tuck the film into the door - try to stick it to the glass by wedging-in a wad of paper cloth too.

13 Spray the film with the soapy water . . .

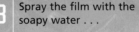

14 . . . then carefully start to squeegee it into place, working from top to bottom. We found that, to get into the corners, it was easier to unscrew the blade from the squeegee, and use that on its own for some of it.

15 You'll end up with a few strips at the bottom, which seemingly will not stick to the glass. Don't panic. First, soak up any excess water at the base of the film, with paper towels. Now using a hot-air gun to very gently warm the film should help to finish drying, and encourage the film to stick. Be careful squeegee-ing the film when it's dry - risk of damage. Don't lift the film off the glass - the adhesive will stick, given time. Persistence pays off.

Fitting a sunstrip

The modern sunstrip, first seen as a lovely green shadeband on Cortinas and Capris back in the 70s, usually bearing imaginative slogans such as 'DAVE AND SHARON'. Just goes to show that some things improve with age.

There are two options to make your car look (and maybe even feel) cooler:

a The sunvisor, a screen tint band inside the screen, which is usually a graduated-tint strip. As this fits inside, there's a problem straight away - the interior mirror. Your Punto mirror may be bonded to the screen, and it seriously gets in the way when trying to fit a wet and sticky (nice!) strip of plastic around it. Go for a sunstrip instead.

b The sunstrip, which is opaque vinyl, colour-matched to the car, fits to the outside of the screen. Much more Sir.

A really wide sunstrip imitates the 'roof chop' look seen on American hot rods, and colour-coded, they can look very effective from the front - plus, of course, you can use the space to advertise your preferred brand of ICE (no, no, NO! Not a good idea!). As it's fitted to the outside of the screen, the sunstrip has a good chance of seriously interfering with your wipers (or wiper, if you've been converted). If this happens to the point where the wipers can't clean the screen, Mr MOT might have a point if he fails your car... The wiper blades may need replacing more often, and the sunstrip itself might start peeling off - still want one? Well, you've got to, really.

01 This is only stuck to the outside, so only the outside of the screen needs cleaning - excellent! Do a good job of cleaning, though - any dirt stuck under the strip will ruin the effect.

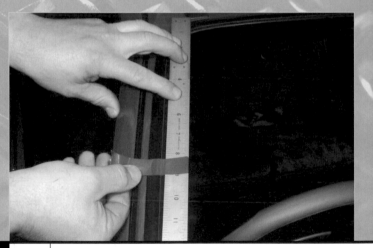

02 With the help of an assistant (if you have one handy), lay the strip onto the car, and decide how far down the screen you're going to go. Legally-speaking, you shouldn't be lower than the wiper swept area - so how much of a 'badboy' are you? If you measure and mark the bottom of the strip with tape, you'll be sure to get it level, even if it's not legal.

Legal eagle
The rule for tinting or otherwise modifying the windscreen is that there must be no more than a 25% light reduction from standard. In theory, this means you can have a sunstrip which covers up to 25% of the screen area, but some MOT testers may see it differently. A sunstrip's got to come down the screen a fair way, to look any sense (otherwise, why bother?). You could argue that accurately measuring and calculating the windscreen area isn't actually that easy, if you get stopped, and anyway, a sunstrip also cuts out harmful glare! If you go so far down the screen that you can't see out, though - well, that's just stupid.

>

03 Trim off the excess strip at this stage - means you'll have less flapping about when you start trying to stick it down.

04 Spray the screen with water (mixed with a drop of washing-up liquid) . . .

05 . . . then peel off the backing, spraying that as well, and wake up your assistant.

06 With one of you either side of the car, stick the strip on to the masking-tape marks.

07 Using a squeegee and some more spray, get the worst of the air bubbles out now - keep the squeegee wet while you do this, or your new strip will get well-scuffed (worst-case, you'll peel it off at the edges). Getting rid of all the tiny air bubbles is time-consuming and pretty boring, honestly, but essential for a decent job.

08 Trimming-up isn't as scary as it might seem. Make sure you've got a really sharp blade and a steady hand, and cut with firm, decisive strokes rather than lots of little nicks - this is especially true when you get to the corners. Using an old plastic store card helps no end tucking-in the edges. Don't let the excess strip stick to the roof or A-pillars while you're trimming - keep peeling it off.

Tricks 'n' tips

If you have trouble getting things trimmed up neatly, remember that you can lift the windscreen rubber slightly (using a small screwdriver), and tuck the edge of the strip underneath, for a really neat fit.

Painting by numbers

This is not the section where we tell you how to respray your entire Punto in a weekend, using only spray cans, okay? Mission Impossible, we ain't. This bit's all about how to spray up your various plasticky bits before final fitting - bits such as door mirrors, light brows, spoilers, splitters - hell, even bumpers if you like. As we've no doubt said before, with anything new, fit your unpainted bits first. Make sure everything fits properly (shape and tidy up all parts as necessary), that all holes have been drilled, and all screws etc are doing their job. Then, and only when you're totally, completely happy with the fit - take them off, and get busy with the spray cans.

01 The first job is to mask off any areas you don't want painted. Do this right at the start, or you could be sorry; on these door mirrors, we decided to mask off just at the lip before the glass, to leave a black unpainted edge - if we hadn't masked it as the very first job, we would've roughed up all the shiny black plastic next, and wrecked the edge finish.

02 Remove any unwanted 'seams' in the plastic, using fine sandpaper or wet-and-dry. Some of these seams look pretty cool, others don't - you decide. Also worth tidying up any other areas you're not happy with, fit-wise, while you're at it.

Especially with 'shiny' plastic, you must rough-up the surface before spray will 'bite' to it, or - it'll flippin' flake off. Just take off the shine, no more. You can use fine wet-and-dry for this (used dry), but we prefer Scotchbrite. This stuff, which looks much like a scouring pad, is available from motor factors and bodyshops, in several grades - we used ultra-fine, which is grey. One advantage of Scotchbrite is that **03** it's a bit easier to work into awkward corners than paper.

Once the surface has been nicely 'roughened', clean up the surface using a suitable degreaser ('suitable' means a type which won't dissolve plastic!). Generally, it's ok to use methylated spirit or cellulose thinners (just don't inhale!), but **04** test it on a not-so-visible bit first, so you don't have a disaster.

Before you start spraying (if it's something smaller than a bumper) it's a good idea to try a work a screw into one of the mounting holes, to use as a **05** 'handle', so you can turn the item to spray all sides.

Another good trick is to use the screw to hang the item up on a piece of string or wire - then **06** you can spin the item round to get the spray into awkward areas.

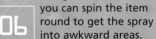
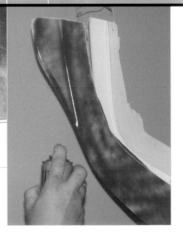

07 If you like a bit of wildlife in your paint, you can't beat the great outdoors. If it's at all windy, you'll end up with a really awful finish and overspray on everything (which can be a real pain to get off). Even indoors, if it's damp weather, you'll have real problems trying to get a shine - some kind of heater is essential if it's cold and wet (but not one with a fan - stirring up the dust is the last thing you want).

08 If you're a bit new at spraying, or if you simply don't want to balls it up, practise your technique first (steady!). Working left-right, then right-left, press the nozzle so you start spraying just before you pass the item, and follow through just past it the other side. Keep the nozzle a constant distance from the item - not in a curved arc. Don't blast the paint on too thick, or you'll have a nasty case of the runs - hold the can about 6 inches away - you're not trying to paint the whole thing in one sweep.

09 Once you've got a patchy 'mist coat' on (which might not even cover the whole thing) - stop, and let it dry (primer dries pretty quickly). Continue building up thin coats until you've got full coverage, then let it dry for half an hour or more.

10 Using 1000- or 1200-grade wet-and-dry paper (used wet), very lightly sand the whole primered surface, to take out any minor imperfections (blobs, where the nozzle was spitting) in the primer. Try not to go through the primer to the plastic, but this doesn't matter too much in small areas.

11 Rinse off thoroughly, then dry the surfaces - let it stand for a while to make sure it's *completely* dry, before starting on the top coat.

12 Make sure once again that the surfaces are clean, with no bits left behind from the drying operations. As with the primer, work up from an initial thin mist coat, allowing time for each pass to dry. As you spray, you'll soon learn how to build a nice shine without runs - any 'dry' (dull) patches are usually due to overspray landing on still-wet shiny paint. Don't worry if you can't eliminate all of these - a light cutting polish will sort it out once the paint's hardened (after several hours).

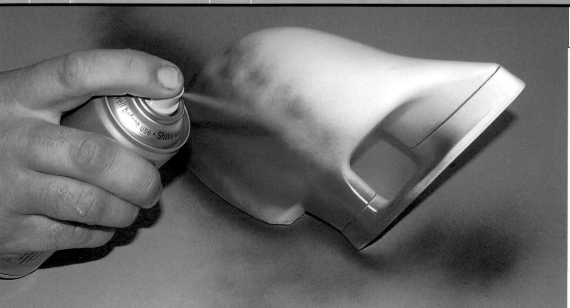

13 Especially with a colour like red (which is notorious for fading easily), it's a good idea to blow on a coat or two of clear lacquer over the top - this will also give you your shine, if you're stuck with a very 'dry' finish. It's best to apply lacquer before the final top coat is fully hardened. The spraying technique is identical, although pro sprayers say that lacquer should be applied pretty thick - just watch those runs! Lacquer also takes a good long while to dry - pick up your item too soon, for that unique fingerprint effect!

There's no way in

De-locking

One way to tidy up the Punto lines is to do away with the door locks, and even the door handles - but be careful. Flushing the rear door handles (on 5-door models) is okay, legally/MOT-speaking, but removing the front door handles will land you in trouble, come MOT time.

Body styling

Construction & Use regs require your car to have an independent mechanical means of door opening from outside (so fire-fighters can get you out, if you stick your all-action Punto on its roof, or in a ditch…) If you must lose the front handles, find some trick mirrors which have door catches built-in, underneath.

At least every Punto (apart from the billy-basic S) has central locking as standard, meaning all you need is a remote alarm with a central locking interface (like the one we fitted in the Security section) and you're sorted.

01 De-locking your Punto doors means removing the lock barrels and plating over the holes. First, remove the door card (see 'Interiors'). When the plastic membrane is pulled back, you'll see a black plate over the access hole to the lock barrel - remove this for better access.

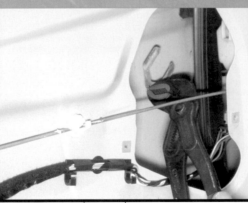

02 Using pliers, slide off the metal retaining clip sideways from the lock barrel . . .

03 . . . and the lock is then free to be removed from the car by hooking it out through the hole. The hole that's left behind is now ready to be filled in. The most DIY-friendly way of plugging this hole is by gluing a metal plate into place behind the hole (see the Tailgate de-locking section, if you don't believe us).

04 Once the glue is dried, all that's left to do is spread some filler over the hole from the outside, prep, prime and spray over the area. You'd never even know you used to have a door lock there! Course, now you've come this far, colour-coding the door handles would be nice…

Remote **locking**

So you can lock and unlock your freshly de-locked doors, you'll need to buy and fit a remote central locking kit, which you can get from several Max Power-advertised suppliers (our Microscan kit is an extra for our chosen alarm, but is pretty typical of what you'll get). If your Punto already has central locking, you're in luck - buy yourself a cheap car alarm, and a central locking interface.

Tricks 'n' tips
If your battery goes flat, you'll be locked out. We ran two thin wires from the battery terminals (with a 10-amp fuse in the live, and the ends insulated), and tucked them away for access from below in an emergency. By connecting a slave battery to these wires (do not try jump-starting), you'll put enough juice into the system to operate the locks, saving you a red face. Think it over.

Central locking **kit**

If your Punto doesn't have central locking as standard, don't despair - there's several kits out there to help you towards your goal. Our project Punto already had central locking, so regrettably there are no Punto-specific photos to show you, but hopefully, the details below, together with your kit's instructions, will help you out.

Before you start fitting your new lock solenoids, it makes sense to test them. Connect them all together as described in your kit's instructions - with power connected to all the solenoids, pull up on the operating plunger of one, and all the rest should pop up too - clever, eh?

Decide where you're going to mount the lock control unit, then identify the various looms, and feed them out to the doors.

The new lock solenoids must be mounted so they work in the same *plane* as the door lock buttons. What this means is it's no good having the lock solenoid plungers moving horizontally, to work a button and rod which operates vertically! Make up the mounting brackets from the metal bits provided in the kit, and fit the solenoids loosely to the brackets, and to the doors.

The kit contains several items which look uncannily like bike spokes - these are your new lock operating rods, which have to be cut to length, then joined onto the old rods using screw clamps. It's best to join the old and new rods at a straight piece of the old rod, so feed the new rod in, and mark it for cutting.

Cut the new rod to the marked length, fit the cut rod to the solenoid, then slip the clamp onto it. Fit the solenoid onto its bracket, and offer the rod into place, to connect to the old rod. Join the new rod and old rod together, and fasten the clamp screws tight. If the clamp screws come loose, you're basically going to be locked out.

Now you can connect up the wires - the easy bit is joining up inside the door. Hopefully, your kit's instructions should be sufficient, but if not, you'll have to resort to the Haynes manual wiring diagrams.

Don't mesh with me, boy

A meshed grille or bumper is just one way to demonstrate who's the daddy of the cruise, and it does a great job of dicing any small insects or rodents foolish enough to wander into the path of your motor. So if you're sick of scrubbing off insect entrails from your paint, and fancy getting even, read on…

Which style of mesh to choose? Classic diamond-shape, or round-hole? In our humble opinion, the round-hole mesh works best on modern roundy-shaped cars (like say, a Corsa) - for everything else, we'll settle for the original and best. But wait - the choice doesn't end with what shape you want. Mesh can now be had in various anodised colours too, to match or contrast with the rest of your chosen paint scheme.

01 Anyone can mesh a hole. Ab-so-lutely anyone - it's dead easy. First, measure your hole, then cut out a roughly-sized piece of mesh, leaving some over the sides to bend around the edges of your hole.

There's loads of ways to secure your mesh. One of the most permanent is to use small self-tapping screws, but this won't always be possible. Our hot-glue gun method worked a treat, as the glue flows into place. You can use mastic (quick-setting, exterior-use type) or even builder's 'no-nails' adhesive, but you squirt on a bead of the stuff, and then have to smooth it on by hand, to 'squidge' it over the mesh. Very meshy - sorry, messy.

02 Of course, holes usually have corners - and some of the sides you'll encounter aren't exactly straight. Make small cuts in the edge of the mesh at strategic points . . .

03 . . . and bending over the edges will be much easier. The main mesh panel will also stay flatter, and you'll be less stressed, too.

04

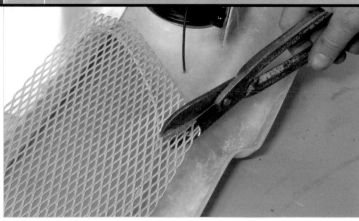

Bumpers 'n' bodykits

If you can't find a kit you like for a Punto, you're not trying - check the various Punto modding websites and chatrooms for ideas if you're stuck. Some people like to mix it up with stuff for the Punto, if they find one kit too limiting - we've heard of Abarth rear spoilers going with Extreme skirts, Cadamuro splitter and a Beast rear valance. Sounds complicated to us, but at least it'll be unique. We went to ProSport UK, who kindly supplied us with a full Combat 2 kit for our Punto.

One thing you should be concerned about is how well it's all going to fit. Even if you're giving the joy of fitting to a bodyshop, they'll still charge you more if your cheap duff kit takes a week longer to fit than expected. Ask around (or check the Punto chat rooms) before splashing the cash.

Front bumper

>>

01 On posher Puntos, the first job is to remove four screws securing a plastic access panel in the wheelarch liner . . .

02 . . . to reveal the foglight. Disconnect the wiring plug, and we're on our way.

>>

03 The main section of the arch liner has to be pulled back, to reach the bumper mounting bolts. Start by removing the three screws along the outside edge of the wheelarch . . .

04 . . . then pull back the liner to reveal two retaining bolts that need to be removed. The first one is located here . . .

05 . . . and the next one's slightly back and up inside the wing, here.

09 Finally, remove the two bolts located either side of the headlight units . . .

10 . . . and the bumper's now free to be lifted off the car and stored in a safe place. Well, you might put it back to standard one day.

11 Try your new bumper in position. You could mesh it now, but we're waiting 'til after it's been sprayed. The ProSport UK Combat 2 front bumper fits as well as the original, which is very unusual for an aftermarket kit. You can re-use the original bumper mounting points - mark where to drill the holes with the bumper on, then remove it for drilling. It really is that easy.

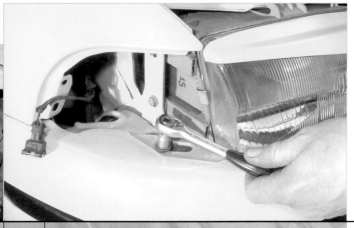

06 Slacken and remove the four screws from the lower edge of the bumper - there are two screws each side.

07 Next, the front indicators have to come out. They're held in by a spring, hooked into a recess on the inner wing - find the looped end of the spring, and pull backwards to unhook it.

08 Pull the light slightly out from the car, then either twist the bulbholder anti-clockwise to free it, or disconnect the bulbholder wiring plug. Once it's removed, you can see a bumper retaining bolt that needs to be slackened and removed. Repeat the process for the opposite indicator unit.

12 An added bonus of using the original mounting points is that you can use the original bolts to fix the bumper in place – you really couldn't ask for more, could you?

13 Finally, some home-made brackets underneath for added staying power completes the fixing on of the new bumper. These are simply strips of alloy (DIY-store brackets) that have been bent to shape and screwed into place.

Rear bumper

To gain considerably better access to the rear bumper mountings, we advise you to jack the car up, remove the wheel and place the car on axle stands, but it's totally up to you. To remove the rear bumper, start by removing the two

01 screws found on the edge of the rear wheelarch.

02 Next, remove the Allen bolt located in the top of the wheelarch.

03 Move to the underside of the bumper now, and remove the four retaining bolts along the bottom edge.

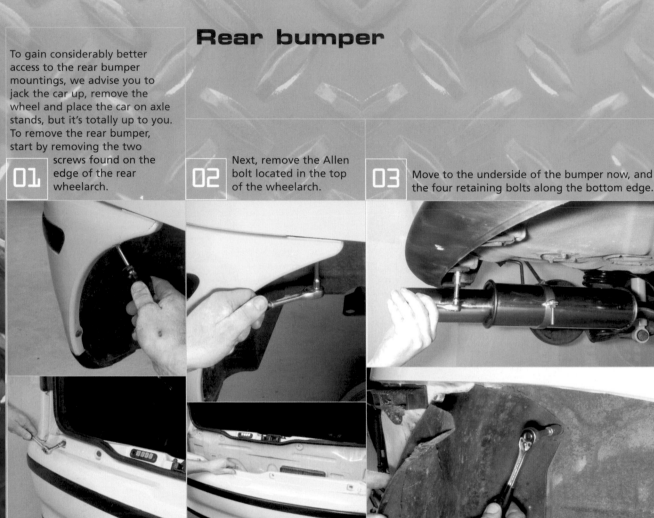

04 Finally, with one hand supporting the weight of the bumper, remove the four upper retaining bolts.

05 The old bumper should now be free to be lifted away from the car, but check first to see that there aren't any electrical plugs/cables that need to be disconnected before removing the bumper.

06 Go back to the wheelarches and remove the piece of arch liner that has been left behind, by removing the two retaining bolts.

07 Before even thinking about fitting your new bumper, give the area a good clean.

08 You may be lucky here and have a bumper that has already been meshed, but this is pretty unlikely (skip to the section on meshing). Time to try it for fit - like the front bumper, the ProSport Combat 2 rear bumper goes straight on, and will use all the original mounting points. What a bonus.

09 All you need to do to fit this particular bumper is arm yourself with a drill, and make holes in the mounting-hole recesses provided in the fibreglass - these being the four holes along the top edge of the bumper . . .

10 . . . and three holes in each wheel arch.

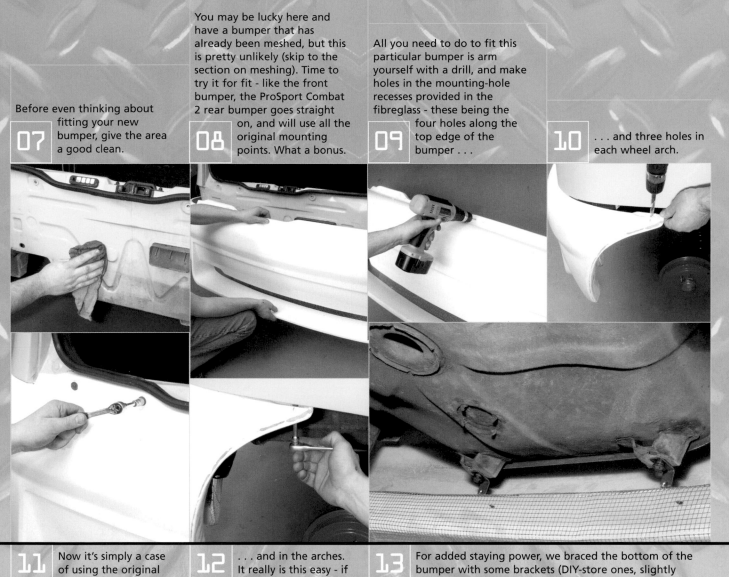

11 Now it's simply a case of using the original bolts/screws to fix the bumper in place, along the top . . .

12 . . . and in the arches. It really is this easy - if you buy a well-made kit like this.

13 For added staying power, we braced the bottom of the bumper with some brackets (DIY-store ones, slightly modified). Align the new brackets with the original bumper lower mounting points, and you can re-use the original bolts. Just bend the brackets to shape, and screw them to the bumper (using self-tappers and U-nuts, like on our side skirts) and the car.

Side skirts

So what's the deal with side skirts, then? Well, they're an 'artificial' way of visually lowering the car, making it seem lower to the ground than it really is, and they also help to 'tie together' the front and rear sections of a full bodykit. This much we know from our magazines. But where did skirts really come from?

As with so much else in modifying, it's a racing-inspired thing. In the late 70s, the Lotus 'ground-effect' F1 cars ran very, very low (for the time) and had side skirts made of rubber (or bristles), to give a flexible seal against the track. With a clear downforce advantage, Lotus blew the opposition away.

So will fitting skirts to your Punto give you race-car levels of downforce, greatly increasing your overtaking chances at the next roundabout? You already know the answer, I'm afraid...

Tricks 'n' tips
Only attempt to carry out procedures such as this one on a dry day. The car will be out of action for a maximum of 24 hours, so make prior arrangements, and try not to drive the car during this time.

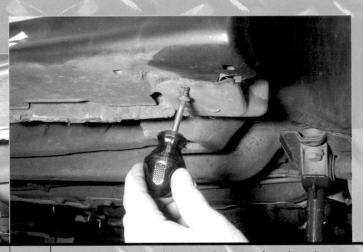

01 Popping the car on axle stands is not absolutely necessary for this, but it does make the job easier with the car higher off the ground. First, there's the old skirt to remove. Unscrew the six retaining bolts located on the underside of the skirt . . .

02 . . . then unscrew and remove the screw found on the underside of the skirt, nearest to the front wheel.

 03 Next we need to gain access to a hidden bolt, accessible only by removing part of the front wheel liner. This is done by removing the two liner retaining screws . . .

04 . . . and drawing the liner away from the arch . . .

05 . . . a spanner can then be used to remove the final retaining bolt.

All that's left now is to prise the side skirt away from the car, using a spatula or similar tool. Take care not to damage the paintwork by putting some cardboard between the car and spatula. The clips that hold the skirt in place are seriously in there, so be prepared to put some white-knuckle effort into it.

06

07 The side skirt is now free to be removed from the car – if it hasn't already fallen to the floor!

Before you go any further, give the bodywork a good clean, as it will be pretty filthy. Even the best bodyshop mastic won't stick on cruddy paint.

08

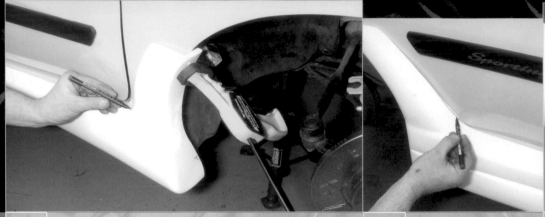

09 Take your new side skirt and offer it into place on the car. Use G-clamps (or a willing assistant) to hold the skirt in place whilst you check out exactly how well the kit fits. Mark any areas that need to be trimmed away. It can be quite time-consuming, but necessary to achieve a good result.

10 When you've trimmed the front end, you might find the rear needs 'adjustment' as well. The ProSport UK Combat 2 kit we're fitting requires very little work at all.

11 The excess fibreglass can be removed using a coarse grade of sandpaper.

To attach the new brackets to the glassfibre, place U-nuts over the holes in the new brackets - this gives the self-tapping screws something to bite into. You can buy U-nuts from any good DIY store or car accessory shop, when you get your self-tappers.

Now the brackets are in place, you can see the rather large gap between the car and the glassfibre. This is totally intentional, by the way - this kit's really going to 'lower' the car a treat.

If you look carefully, you'll see that we've put our brackets in line with the old mountings for the original side trim, enabling us to re-use the original mounting holes and bolts. We amaze ourselves, sometimes.

15

16

17

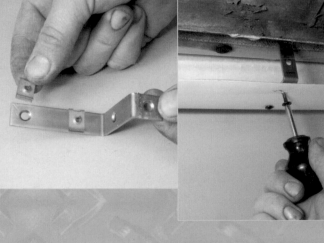

12 When you're satisfied the skirt is trimmed to perfection, it's time to work out exactly how you're going to fix it in place for good. Start by securing the skirt to the doorstep - three screws should do it.

13 Drill two more holes for screws, in both front and rear wheel arches.

14 Finally, a couple of home-made brackets, fixed to the underside of the car, should hold the side skirt in place nicely. The side skirt will have to be in place on the car whilst these brackets are measured and made, but then must come off the car later to have a bead of adhesive applied.

Now after all that fixing the skirt in place, whip it off the car and apply a good bead of adhesive to the areas that will have contact with the car. In this case, not the bottom edge of the skirt, as there's at least a two-inch gap between skirt and sill! This might look like silicone bath sealant, but it's proper bodyshop mastic (okay, so it's usually **18** black, but who cares?).

You're now ready to permanently fix the skirt in place. Pop the skirt into position and secure with G-clamps or get a mate to hold it, whilst you go around and start screwing the kit down. Run your finger along the join between kit and car, so that any excess adhesive that oozed out will fill any gaps to **19** give a smoother, cleaner finish.

Don't despair if the adhesive gets on the paintwork - if it does, wipe it clean straightaway using brake cleaner, or other suitable solvent. Once the brackets and screws are in place, give the mastic plenty of time to do its thing - most take at least 24 hours **20** to become fully effective. Now you just gotta get it sprayed - over to you!

Tricks 'n' tips
Notice our mechanic's wearing gloves for the messy stuff with mastic? He's not usually too bothered about keeping his hands clean, so there must be a reason. This stuff is a real pig to get off your hands (and black mastic's worse, if anything), so a pair of latex gloves is a very sound investment.

Spoil your Punto rotten

This spoiler comes in kit form, in an MFI-stylee. Self-assembly isn't hard, though there will be some holes to drill, to join on the endplates. On some kits, the holes are at least pre-marked. **01**

When it comes to fitting the endplates to the main wing, drill and fit one screw first, then align again before drilling through for the second. **02**

A must for any Punto, a rear spoiler makes a very clear statement to the car you just passed - do not mess. Our very fine Combat 2 spoiler from ProSport UK should do the trick. Fitting a spoiler is actually one of the easier jobs in modifying - just take plenty of time making sure you've got it straight, which means lots of eyeing-up, measuring, and getting a second opinion from a mate. Before you drill any holes, make sure you can actually use those holes to fit nuts and bolts through - you'll usually also need some sealant, to keep water out of your boot. Some spoilers aren't designed to be bolted on, but you can achieve surprisingly-solid results using good-quality mastic alone (provided you wait for it to go off).

03 Go to the car now, and put some masking tape over the tailgate area where the spoiler will fit. Measure and mark the centre spot, then the spoiler can be offered into place and lined up. When you're absolutely positive the spoiler is on centrally, mark the mounting holes ready for drilling.

04 This is no time for nerves - drill some holes in your tailgate with confidence.

05 To make room to fit a retaining nut on the spoiler mounting bolt, it's necessary to enlarge the hole inside the tailgate, just in the first 'skin' of metal.

06 Before the spoiler gets bolted up on the roof for good, rub down the endplates that make contact with the car, so they match the profile of the tailgate top surface. All that's left now is some finishing off when it goes to the bodyshop for spraying. When the spoiler's been painted, and is ready for final fitting, a little sealant round the mounting bolts will keep the water out.

Wheelarch
mods

The law states that your wide rubber shouldn't be so wide that it sticks out from your arches, and the MOT crew will not be impressed if your new rubber's rubbing, either. This presents something of a problem, if you're determined to get 17s or 18s on, especially if the car's also having a radical drop job (like our Punto, on coilovers). If you've got rubbing problems on 15s or 16s, something's very wrong. Check that your wheels are the right offset (see *'Wheels & tyres'*), or chat to your wheel supplier about spacers.

Sometimes, all you need to stop those nasty grinding noises is a small amount of violence. Any non-vital protrusions into the under-arch area can be trimmed off or flattened with a hammer. Also, try removing those (oh-so-practical) wheelarch liners.

Serious wheelarch mods are best done at a bodyshop. Having the arches professionally rolled, using the proper tool, should only cost about £50 per arch (assuming they haven't also got rust or filler to deal with as well). Less satisfactory would be having the arch edges cut or ground off - this leaves a bare-metal edge, and encourages rust (as well as weakening the wings).

The best answer to arches which just aren't roomy enough is, of course, a wide-arch bodykit. And bank loans are so cheap these days.

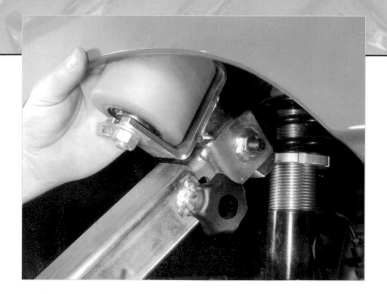

Bonnet vents

Once you've got your bodykit on, it's only natural you'll want a bonnet vent, isn't it? Respect.

But this is one scary job to tackle yourself, unless you're really that good, or that brave. Plenty of options - you can get little louvres stamped in as well, to complement your Evo, Impreza, Integrale or F50 main vent. And, like Focus side repeaters, Focus WRC bonnet vents have now been fitted to everything from Novas upwards (so you may want to scope around for something more original). Speaking of which, there's even been a feature car with a bonnet scoop from a (sensible) Kia Sedona people carrier! Truly, anything goes.

A less-scary option is to buy a ready-made, pre-vented bonnet - fitting one of these is about as easy as it gets. But we like a challenge - not only are we fitting a vent ourselves, it's an F50 vent (one of the biggest you can get). Game on.

There are two main ways of fitting a bonnet vent, and both include chopping your bonnet about. The first option is to cut a complete-vent-size hole in the bonnet, and fit it up from below - this way, the vent is sunk into the bonnet and doesn't stand proud. The second is to place the vent on top of the bonnet, cut out the shapes of any recessed parts, so that the vent actually sits on the bonnet. The process you choose will to a certain extent depend on the size and thickness of the vent you're fitting. Option 1 for fitting a vent is the preferred way, but not always easy at home in the garage. We're going to show you Option 2.

01 Start by creating a full-size card template of the bonnet vent.

02 Next mark the areas of the vent that are going to be recessed down through the bonnet.

. . . you should now be left with something that looks like this. So far, all you've done is create a piece of card with holes in, and drawn on your bonnet - both processes which are reversible. The next bit isn't, really - are you up for the challenge of cutting large holes in your bonnet?

03 The template must now be put into place on the bonnet. Take your time to measure the bonnet, and place the vent centrally (and straight!).

04 Hold the template in place with masking tape, and mark the holes for cutting . . .

05

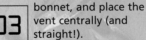

06 Taking a jigsaw with the right blade, begin cutting out the holes. This is harder than it looks - at times you'll be cutting through the bonnet braces inside. Prop the bonnet open slightly using some wood (so your blade doesn't hit any engine bits), and put something over the engine to protect it from the shower of swarf it's about to receive.

07 When the holes have been cut, try the vent in place and it should sit nicely on the bonnet. If you've been holding your breath until now, allow yourself one sigh of relief.

08 Next job is to find a way of securing the vent in place whilst the adhesive, which you'll be adding later on, gets to work. Screws are the easiest option, so start by drilling a series of holes along the edges of the vent.

09 Now drill the corresponding holes in the bonnet. The easiest way of doing this is to put the vent on centrally, hold it still (or tape it in place) and drill down through the holes in the vent and into the bonnet.

10 Add some self-tapping screws and washers, and that vent's going nowhere . . .

. . . or is it? Once you've gone to all that bother of fixing the vent in place, now you have to remove it. It's time to apply a nice thick bead of heavy-duty adhesive (proper bodyshop mastic, please). At the end of the day, this bond is what's going to be holding the vent in place, so don't be stingy - give the whole area a hefty squirt.

11

Once the bond has been applied, the vent can be put back into place and screwed in securely until the glue has dried. Any excess that squeezes out can be smoothed around the edge of the vent with a finger.

12

Once the adhesive has dried, we're able to remove the screws - as if by magic, the vent stays where it is. The really time-consuming bit is smoothing the vent into the bonnet - lots of filing-down the edges, lots of filler. We gave the job to our brand new bodyshop at the Haynes Motor Museum. Once this stage is complete, the bonnet's ready to be primed and painted.

13

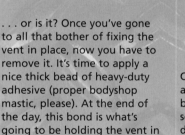

Respraying

Not happy with your Punto's 'pensioner blue' paint? Time to call in the pros. There's no such thing as a simple DIY respray (not one that'll look good afterwards, at any rate). We just thought you'd like to see some of the stages involved.

01 Before we get anywhere near the paint cans, it's out with the masking tape and brown paper - lots of it. All we're doing here is masking up to spray the flushed tailgate, but it still takes ages - if it doesn't, you're doing it wrong.

02 Pro sprayers often call masking 'bagging-up', and this shot shows why. Remember - paint will find its way in anywhere, so all-round masking (putting the rest of the car 'in a bag') is the only answer.

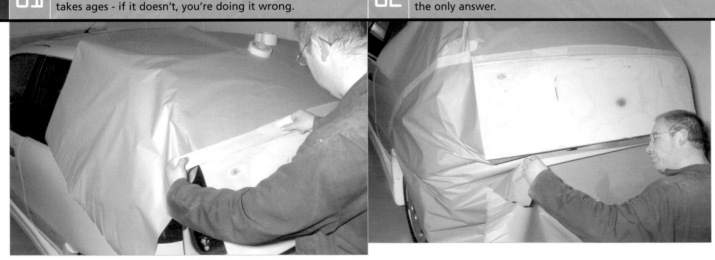

03 Now the main spray area's completely covered, so we're finished? No way - paint will hang in the air for ages, and then fall quite a distance from the bit you're spraying. It dries as it falls, so it won't necessarily stick to anything, but it still makes a heck of a mess. Companies like 3M specialise in producing easy-to-use dust sheets which work almost like cling film.

04 Mixing the paint is an important, but often overlooked, stage in any spraying process - even ambient temperatures have a bearing on the final paint mix. Topcoats and lacquer especially have complex mixing ratios for the thinners, hardener, activator, and any 'flex' additives for bumpers and such - get it wrong, and even top-notch paint like this won't work.

05 Making sure the paint surface is clean between steps is another often-overlooked essential item. Panel wipe does exactly what it says on the tin, taking off any oils and greases, leaving a ready-to-spray finish. A water-based wash is favourite, as solvent-based products can lift the paint (or react with the next coat).

The final stage before spraying is a wipe over using tack-rags (net-like material, impregnated with resin - very sticky, picks up any bits).

06

Okay, so this is just a boring coat of grey primer. If our Punto was getting a custom paint job, however, this might have been a base coat. With pearlescent and 'flip' paints, the base coat makes a huge difference to the shade of the final topcoat, and choosing the right one is vital.

07

After a quick rubdown, we're ready for the topcoat. There's very few colours where a difference in shade doesn't show, but yellow's definitely one that's got to be right. Can't wait to see the finished result!

08

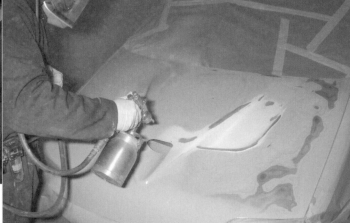

Lights
& bulbs

Being scene
Lights - one of the easiest and coolest ways to trick up your Punto. Several options here, so we'll start at the front, and work back.

Headlights

Almost nothing influences the look of your Punto more than the front end, so the headlights play a crucial role.

What's available?

The popular cheap option is stick-on headlight 'brows', which do admittedly give the rather bland Punto front end a tougher look. The brows are best sprayed to match the car, before fitting - most are fitted using stick-on Velcro pads. Street-cred on the cheap, and (if you choose the Fox-style brows) a cheap alternative to a proper 'badboy' bonnet.

Another cheap option is again stick-on - this time, it's adhesive covers which give the twin-headlight look. This is basically a sheet of vinyl/plastic (shaped to the headlights, and colour-matched to your car) with two holes cut in it. Dead easy to fit, but dare we say, a bit tacky? Just our opinion. A cheap and simple way to get close to the twin-light look.

If you want tinted headlights, you could try spray-tinting them, but go easy on the spray. Turning your headlights from clear glass to non-see-through is plain daft, even if it's done in the name of style. A light tint is quite effective, and gives you the chance to colour-match to your Punto. With tinted headlights, you'd be wise to tint those clear front indicators too, of course.

Pub trivia

The popular twin-headlight look was derived from a cunning tweak first employed in the Touring Cars, years ago. Some teams homologated a twin-headlight unit, but for racing, turned one pair of the 'headlights' into air inlets, to direct air from the front of the car to brake ducts or into the engine air intakes, as required. Think about it - why else would the touring cars bother with headlight mods? Until recently, there were no night races!

Another 'headlight' option sometimes featured on Puntos actually belongs in the bodywork section - it's the 'badboy' bonnet. By cunningly welding-in a couple of triangular plates to your standard Punto bonnet, a bodyshop (or handy DIY-er) can create a really mean look, using just the standard lights. Excellent. Still on the subject of bodywork, you'll need a few minor body mods if you fancy fitting some Punto Mk 2 headlights to a Mk 1, but it's far from impossible, and really improves the look.

Getting more expensive, we're looking at complete replacement lights - 'proper' twin-headlights, available as a kit from the French company Morette. Typically around £300 a set at time of writing, these are for those who're seriously into their cars - maximum cred, and no-one's gonna accuse you of owning a 'boring' Fiat ever again! The light surrounds have to be sprayed to match your car, and fitting is not without some difficulties, but the finished result is SO worth it.

Headlight brows

This is the cheap 'n' cheerful approach, and it really doesn't get much simpler than this. This is even a mod you can 'undo' easily, if your MOT geezer objects. So what do you get? Two bits of triangular plastic, and two strips of Velcro - how hard can this be?

01 Before attempting to fit the light brows to your car, make sure you offer them into place first, just to check that they fit. No major trimming should be needed - have they sent you the right ones?

02 Brows would look kinda odd if you didn't paint them – so this is the first job. Begin by roughing up the surface of the brow using Scotchbrite (or some wet-and-dry).

07 Whilst the paint dries, you can get on and prep the headlight ready for the brows. This means giving it a good clean with a degreaser (brake cleaner again!).

08 For ease when fitting the light brow, we removed the front indicator. The indicator unit's held in by a spring, hooked into a recess on the inner wing - find the looped end of the spring, and pull backwards to unhook it.

09 Pull the light slightly out from the car, then either twist the bulbholder anti-clockwise to free it, or disconnect the bulbholder wiring plug.

10 Now that our paint's had time to dry, we're gently raising the temperature of the rear of the light brow, using a heat gun set to its lowest setting. This helps the next stage . . .

03 A quick clean with a suitable degreaser will help the paint stick better, so do this now. Brake cleaner is an ace degreasing agent, but meths works well, too.

04 Next, you're ready for the first stage of painting – that's plastic primer. Read the can for instructions - usually you mix and warm the paint by shaking the can, then spray at the recommended distances. Two light coats of paint should cover the brow nicely - avoid paint-runs by building up thin layers of paint/primer. Leave to dry for the stated time.

05 Once the primer is completely dry, check the finish - this is usually okay to carry on and spray straight over, but if you see blobs or bits in the paint, a quick rub-down with fine-grade wet-and-dry will give a better final finish.

06 Time to apply the topcoat. It's always best if you can try and find the paint description and code, printed on a sticker inside the tailgate (or in the handbook), and buy paint directly from Fiat – it will be the best colour-match, and will give the best results. Remember, avoid paint runs and leave plenty of time to dry.

11 ... which is sticking on the Velcro pads that hold the brow in place on the headlight. Don't separate the two 'halves' of Velcro - just peel off one of the backing papers, and stick firmly. You'll need to trim the Velcro into shorter strips, to get the top and bottom edges of the brow covered.

12 Carefully raise the temperature of the headlight glass in the same way as the brow . . .

13 . . . then peel off the remaining backing papers . . .

14 . . . and you're ready to stick the brow in place. Take your time lining it up - that adhesive's well-sticky, and you really want to get it on there right, first-time. Refit the indicator, and the headlight makeover is complete.

Morette lights

01 Right - let's start by ripping out the old lights. Not a bad idea to disconnect the battery at this point. The first job is to remove the indicators, which we covered in fitting the headlight brows earlier. The headlights are held in by three bolts - two are obvious from above, but the third's hiding in the indicator hole.

02 Withdraw the light as far as possible, bearing in mind it's still connected at the back . . .

07 You can, of course, choose when you're going to colour-code your headlight surrounds, but it makes sense to get them sprayed early. Just four screws hold each surround on, but two are underneath once the light's fitted.

08 Fitting the motor to the new light's hardly a challenge - engage the balljoint by pressing it home until it clicks, then twist the motor into position.

09 So is wiring this lot up a complete nightmare? Hardly - Morette lights have always been one of the easiest modding parts to fit, in our humble opinion. Everything's provided, and it all mates up to the stock wiring like a dream. First, plug together the new sections of loom provided . . .

10 . . . then connect the spade connector onto the new sidelight bulb.

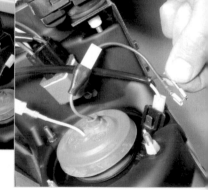

03 . . . but not for much longer. If your Punto's as posh as our Sporting, you may have a headlight adjuster motor plug to disconnect . . .

04 . . . and you'll at least have a main light supply wiring plug to release. No more gakky standard headlights for you! So do you keep them, to put the car back to stock for selling-on, or get them down to the next car boot?

05 One of the bits to be recycled off the old lights is the adjustment motor (if you've got one). This has a ball-and-socket joint inside, which is a bit stiff to detach - the easy bit is twisting the motor from the back of the light.

06 Once it's off, Morette instruct you to set the motor rod so it sticks out of the motor by 32 mm. Not a problem - all you need's a crosshead screwdriver.

They're so thoughtful, they even provide a relay which gives you a live feed for any fogs or spots. We didn't need this, and rather than have a live wire hanging loose, we chopped off the ring terminal and crimped on an insulated female bullet, in case we get the urge for more wattage in future.
11

Time to see how the new lights fit. No surprises here - Morettes are a quality item, and all the original mountings line right up. We like.
12

The new wiring loom fitted to each light can now be plugged into the car's original wiring. Yes, that's all there is to it - just connect up the main light feeds . . .
13

 . . . and the headlight adjuster motors (if fitted). These things make such a huge difference to the looks, it almost doesn't matter if they don't work, does it? Just kidding - you'll be smiling, same as us.
14

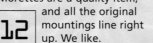

Headlight bulbs

Make your Punto look like an Audi or a Beemer, the easy way. Bad-weather and 'blue' headlight bulbs are an excellent way to boost headlight performance, and are perfect with other blue LED accessories like washer jets and number plate screws. The blue bulbs you buy in most accessory shops will be legal, 60W/55 bulbs, and are no problem. Don't be tempted to buy the mega-powerful bulbs you can get from rallying suppliers (any over 60W/55 are in fact illegal for use in this country) - as with all other non-standard lights, the boys in blue will love pulling you over for a word about this, so ask before you buy.

Even if you're not bothered about the legality of over-powerful bulbs (and you might well argue that being more powerful is the whole point of fitting), there's other problems with monster bulbs.

First, they give off masses of heat, and loads of people have melted their headlights before they found this out. Don't believe us? Try fitting some 100W/90s and put your hand in front of the light, close to the glass. Hot, isn't it? The excess heat these bulbs generate will damage the headlights eventually, either by warping the lens, burning off the reflective coating, or melting the bulbholders. Maybe all three.

The increased current required to work big bulbs has also been known to melt wiring (this could lead to a fire) and will almost certainly burn out your light switch. There's no headlight relay fitted as standard, so the wiring and switch were designed to cope only with the current drawn by standard-wattage bulbs; if you're going for high power, a relay must be fitted (much as you'd have to, to fit foglights or spots).

Tricks 'n' tips
Put the old bulbs in the glovebox - carrying spare bulbs is a good way to get a let-off from Plod, if they stop you for having a bulb gone. Be smart. Carry spares.

Front fog/spotlights

Extra lights are useful for adding features to the Punto's rather bland front end, even if they are a bit harder to fit than mesh. Most front bumpers have the facility for one or more pairs of lights, so it's gotta be done, really.

If you're fitting fogs, they must be wired in to work on dipped-beam only, so they must go off on main beam. The opposite is true for spotlights. Pop out the main light switch (or pull down the fusebox) and check for a wire which is live only when the dipped beams are on. The Haynes wiring diagrams will help here - on our Punto, it was a grey/red wire we needed, with the left/right beams being fed by fuses 4 and 5 (pull the fuses to check you've got the right wires).

Once you've traced a suitable wire, this is used as the live (+ve) feed for your foglight relay. Did we mention you'll need a relay? You'll need a relay. A four-pin one will do nicely. Splice a new wire onto the feed you've found, and feed it through to the engine (use one of the bulkhead grommets). Decide where you'll mount the relay (next to the battery seems obvious) and connect the new wire onto terminal 86.

For your other relay connections, you'll need an earth to terminal 85 (plenty of good earth spots around the battery). You also need

a fused live supply (buy a single fuseholder, and a 15 or 20-amp fuse should be enough) and take a new feed straight off the battery positive connection - this goes to terminal 30 on your relay.

Terminal 87 on your relay is the live output to the fogs - split this into two wires, and feed it out to where the lights will go. Each foglight will also need an earth - either pick a point on the body next to each light, or run a pair of wires back to the earth point you used earlier for your relay. Simple, innit?

With the wiring sorted, now you'd best fit the lights. Over to you. Most decent foglights come with some form of mounting brackets - you must be able to adjust the aim, even if only slightly. To look their best, hopefully your new lights can slot into pre-cut holes in your new front bumper/bodykit.

To connect the wiring to the lights, you'll probably need to splice on your wires from terminal 87 to the new wiring plugs which came with the lights - not too difficult. Plug it all together, and test - you should now have some rather funky fogs!

Front indicators

Tragically, some Puntos came with orange front indicators. There's just no excuse for this kind of thing. Luckily, companies such as ABC Design produce clear replacements, which just go straight in (see the light brows section for how to swap out the indicators). Though our Punto already had clears, we noticed the new clear lights had just an extra touch of shiny chrome at the rear. It's not much, but at least it's not standard.

Side repeaters

There's a range of 'standard' colours that side reps come in, but most people go for clear or smoked, to colour-code with their rear clusters.

Side repeaters must still show an orange light. The stock bulbs are clear, so make sure you get orange bulbs too.

Side repeaters are available in many different shapes (triangular Focus-style side reps, for instance). But the standard ovals are recessed into the wings, so making other shapes fit properly may need a bit of bodywork.

Or how about ditching the repeaters altogether, and get some tasty Merc-style mirrors, with side reps built-in? You could smooth your front wings, then…

Don't just prise the old light without thinking - it's a good way to wreck your wing. Using a small screwdriver (and some paper to protect the paint), lift the front edge of the light and press it backwards, then

01 carefully unhook the light out from the front.

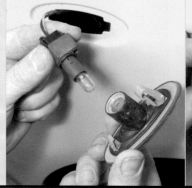

02 The old orange lens just twists off the bulbholder. Incidentally, while you're swapping these lights over, don't let the bulbholder fall back inside the wing panel, or you'll swear. A lot. If it's not just a simple swap over, tape the bulbholder to the wing.

03 With virtually any replacement side reps, you'll need a new bulb (check whether your chosen items come with new bulbs - not all do). Side reps still have to show an amber light, so if you've chosen clear lenses, you need an amber bulb. Pull the old one straight out, push in the new one.

04 If you've ordered proper replacement lights for a Punto (not 'universal' items), your new clear/smoked/whatever lens should twist straight onto the Fiat bulbholder. These fitted just fine (thanks, ABC Design).

05 With the bulbholder in place, the new clear lens just hooks into the hole in the wing - a perfect fit. How much easier could they make it?

Rear lights

Punto rear lights are just mahoosive. Really, really big. What we're actually trying to say here is - choose your rear lights carefully, as they will make quite a statement. The choice is usefully large, with all the popular styles catered for - afterburners, Lexus, smoked... There's also companies who'll sell you rear light masks, which is another cheaper option. Our 3D-style rear clusters came to us courtesy of ABC Design.

Light legality

Lots of Punto rear clusters there may be, but - often, they're not UK-legal (even lights which are E-marked sometimes have no rear fogs or reflectors). Mr. Plod is well-informed on this point, and those sexy rear lights are way too big a come-on for him to ignore.

You can buy stick-on reflectors, but these are about as sexy as NHS specs, so there's no easy answer on this. You'd have to be pretty unlucky to get pulled just for having no rear reflectors, but don't say we didn't warn you. And what happens if your car gets crunched, parked at night with no reflectors fitted? Will your insurance try and refuse to pay out? You betcha.

If you've got a rad rear bumper planned, why not cut a hole in your new rear bumper/mesh, and find a cool-looking rear fog to mount inside (the Peugeot 206 unit's pretty sweet). If you don't mind a bit extra work, source an exhaust tailpipe trim roughly the same size as your existing single pipe, mount it on the opposite side of the car, and fit a round foglight inside the end.

Any questions on light legality? Why not check out the ABC Design website tech tips page, at www.abcdesignltd.com - if you've any questions after that, you can e-mail them. We're so good to you.

Light tinting

01 Spraying your lights is a top idea if funds are too tight for replacements, or if you simply don't fancy paying loadsamoney for illegal lights which also don't fit very well. The first job before spraying is to get the old lights clean - we used meths, which works well enough to get off all the old silicone products and polish residue.

02 As with most spray-painting, the trick is to get the stuff on evenly, which means applying light coats. Blasting it on too thick will give you the runs, which is never pleasant. How thick is too thick? A couple of light coats might be too subtle a look for you, but don't go too mad if you want to avoid attention from the Law.

Rear light clusters

01 Open the boot, then prise out the plastic cap from the rear pillar trim panel, and the one lower down in the boot carpet.

02 Next, using the special tool provided with the car, unscrew the two cluster retaining screws.

03 Here's a shot of the lower retaining nut being removed. Keep these odd-looking pieces of hardware in a safe place.

04 Next from outside the car, lift the light unit out of the recess. You'll see that there's a wiring plug that needs to be disconnected before the unit is totally free to be lifted out.

05 We're fitting some rather rad new clusters from our friends at ABC Design - these are the 'bazooka-style' lights. First job in the swap-over story is unscrewing the bulbholders from the old lights (four screws) . . .

06 . . . then lift 'em out. It's worth checking all the bulbs before fitting the bulbholder into the new light - if any of the bulb glasses look black or silvered inside, this normally means the bulb ain't got long to go. Change any suspect bulbs now, if you've got spares handy.

07 Transfer the bulbholder to the new light, and screw it on. Simple. The new light can now be fitted, just the same way the old one came off. Before it goes in, clean the car bodywork round the light hole, and check that the new light has a decent foam seal fitted, to keep the water out - if not, use a little silicone to seal it. Don't want water with our ICE, do we?

Wheels
& tyres

Your most **important decision** ever?

You don't need us to tell you just how important wheels and tyres are on your motor. They're a hefty investment, so are well worth taking your time over. Get the right style, and your car can turn from average to amazing in a matter of minutes. Get the selection wrong, and not only will it affect the looks of car, it can seriously hurt your finances.

Due to the wheel-size limitations imposed by the Punto's tight rear arches, it's important to choose a wheel that looks bigger than it is, with spokes right out to the rim edges (unless you're really going for the small-wheel Euro-look). Advice on which particular wheels to buy would be a waste of space, since the choice is so huge, and everyone will have their own favourites. For what it's worth, though, something in a multi-spoker usually looks sweet on a Punto, so maybe some OZ's?. For a dash of Italian style, many people turn to Momo's wheel offerings, and most Mille Miglia rims seem to suit the car, too. This year's look is chrome, and the US-based sites have plenty to see (Motorsport International, for starters, and DM Tech America). Even Wolfrace have recently jumped on the chrome bandwagon - or try Cam chromes for another value choice.

One point not to overlook when choosing wheels is the wheel offset - more on this later. More of an issue on the Punto is the wheel bolt pattern, which is a highly-unusual 4 x 98, and virtually unique to Fiat. When ordering your wheels, make sure you mention they're for a Fiat Punto at an early stage. A more-common 'next size up' in bolt patterns is 4 x 100, but don't assume you'll be able to make these fit a Punto using your standard wheel bolts. If your dream rims are only available in 4 x 100, you'll need to order some 'wobbly bolts' (sometimes known as an 'alloy wheel fitting kit') at the same time. These special bolts have a floating collar, which locks into the wheel, and allows you to safely fit 4 x 100 wheels to a 4 x 98 car - they should be available from most good wheel suppliers.

Lead us not into
temptation

Before going any further into which wheels are right for you, a word about insurance and security. Fitting tasty alloys to your Punto is one of the first and best ways to make it look cool. It follows, therefore, that someone with dubious morals might very well want to unbolt them from your car while you're not around, and make their own car look cool instead (or simply sell them, to buy spot cream and drugs).

Since fitting a set of top alloys is one of the easiest bolt-on ways to trick up any car, it's no surprise that the market in stolen alloys is as alive and kicking as it currently is - your wheels will also look very nice on any number of other cars, and the owners of those cars would love to own them at a fraction of the price you paid… It's not unknown for a set of wheels to go missing just for the tyres - if you've just splashed out on a set of fat Yokohamas, your wheels look even more tempting, especially if you've got a common-size tyre.

Tell your insurance company what you're fitting. What will probably happen is that they'll ask for the exact details, and possibly a photo of the car with the wheels on. Provided you're happy to then accept that they won't cover the extra cost of the wheels if they get nicked (or if the whole car goes), you may find you're not charged a penny more, especially if you've responsibly fitted some locking bolts. Not all companies are the same, though - some charge an admin fee, and yes, some will start loading your premium. If you want the rims covered, it's best to talk to a company specialising in modified cars, or you could be asked to pay out the wheel cost again in premiums. The daftest thing you can do is say nothing, and hope they don't find out - we don't want to go on about this, but there are plenty of documented cases where insurance companies have refused to pay out altogether, purely on the basis of undeclared alloy wheels.

How **cheap** are you?

Hopefully, you'll be deciding which wheels to go for based on how they look, not how much they cost, but inevitably (for most ordinary people at least), price does become a factor. Surely buying a cheaper wheel must have its pitfalls? Well, yes - and some of them may not be so obvious.

Inevitably, cheaper wheels = lower quality, but how does this show up? Cheap wheels are often made from alloys which are more 'porous' (a bit like a sponge, they contain microscopic holes and pockets of air). Being porous has two main disadvantages for a wheel, the main one being that it won't be able to retain air in the tyres. The days of tyres with inner tubes are long gone (and it's illegal to fit tubes to low-profile tyres), so the only thing keeping the air in are the three 'walls' of the tyre, with the fourth 'wall' being the inside of the wheel itself. If you like keeping fit by pumping up your tyres every morning, go ahead - the rest of us will rightly regard this as a pain, and potentially dangerous (running tyres at low pressure will also scrub them out very effectively - what was that about saving money?).

Porous wheels also have difficulty in retaining their paint, lacquer, or chrome finish, with flaking a known problem, sometimes after only a few months. This problem is made worse by the fact that porous wheels are much harder to clean (brake dust gets ingrained into the wheels more easily) - and the more you scrub, the more the lacquer comes off.

The final nail in the coffin for cheap wheels is that they tend to corrode (or 'fizz') more. This not only ruins the looks if visible from outside, but if you get corrosion between the wheel and the hub, you won't even be able to take the damn things off! Yes seriously, grown men with all the specialist tools in the world at their disposal will be scratching their heads when faced with wheels which simply **will not** come off.

Buying an established, popular make of wheel has another hidden benefit, too. Choosing a popular wheel will mean more suppliers will stock it, and the manufacturers themselves will make plenty of them. And if you're unlucky enough to have an accident (maybe a slide on a frosty road) which results in non-repairable damage to one wheel, you're going to need a replacement. If you've chosen the rarest wheels on the planet, you could be faced with having to replace a complete set of four, to get them all matching... A popular wheel, even if it's a few years old, might be easier to source, even second-hand.

The Sunday morning ritual

It's a small point maybe, but you'll obviously want your wheels to look as smart as possible, as often as possible - so how easy are they going to be to clean?

The real multi-spokers and BBS-style 'wires' are hell to clean - a fiddly toothbrush job - do you really want that much aggro every week? The simpler the design, the easier time you'll have. For those who like nothing better than counting their spokes, though, there are several really good products out there to make your life less of a cleaning nightmare.

Bolt from the blues

Don't forget about locking wheel bolts (see *'Hold on to your wheels'* further on) - bargain these into a wheel/tyre package if you're buying new. You may also need some 'wobbly bolts' if your new rims are the (wrong) 4 x 100 bolt pattern.

A word of warning about re-using your existing wheel bolts, should you be upgrading from steel wheels. Most steel-wheel bolts are not suitable for use with alloy wheels (and vice-versa, incidentally). Make sure you ask about this when buying new wheels, and if necessary, bargain a set of bolts into the price. Most bolts for use with alloys will have a washer fitted, for two very good

reasons - 1) the bolt will pull through the wheel hole without it, and 2) to protect the wheel finish.

Another point to watch for is that the new wheel bolts are the correct length for your fitment, taking into account whether you've fitted spacers or not. Bolts that are too short are obviously dangerous, and ones that are too long can foul on drum brakes, and generally get in the way of any turning activities. If in doubt, ask the retailer for advice. Always check that the wheels turn freely once they've been put on, and investigate any strange noises before you go off for a pose.

Other options

If you're on a really tight budget, and perhaps own a real 'basic' model Punto, don't overlook the possibility of fitting a discarded set of standard alloys (a set of Sporting or GT rims would do). Most Italian car makers use the same wheel bolt pattern, so even if you get offered a set of wheels off an obscure Lancia, providing they're four-stud fitting, they should go on.

If the Fiat range of wheels is too limiting, you'll need to turn your attention to (believe it or not) the Japanese. Most Far Eastern car makers fit alloys with a 4 x 100 bolt pattern - while this isn't the same as Fiat, it's close enough to be an option (providing you buy a set of 'wobbly bolts' to go with them). Other manufacturers who use 4 x 100 are VW, Renault and Vauxhall (but Vauxhall alloys probably won't be the correct offset, and should be avoided).

Tricks 'n' tips
When you have your new wheels balanced, make sure the fast-fit centre knows to use stick-on weights, inside the wheel (not on the rim edge) - old-type knock-on lead weights look lame on the outer wheel edges, and on the inner edges may foul the suspension. Stick-on weights are, however, notorious for falling off easily, even when applied to pristine new alloys.

Size matters

For us Brits, biggest is best - there are Puntos out there with 17s and up. And yes, the mags all say you can't be seen with anything less than 17-inchers. In Europe (and especially Germany) they're mad for the small-wheel look, still with seriously dropped suspension of course.

While the Punto will take 7.5 x 17-inch rims with only fairly minor work needed on the rear arches, remember that 17s won't do wonders for the ride or handling (though the extra tread area might come in handy for traction, on a GT). If you're bothered about how your Punto takes the bends, stick to 15s or 16s instead. Providing the rest of the car's up together, get the car low (35 to 40 mm drop) and you'll still get respect. A comment we saw on one chat room was "get 17s for the look, 15s if you still wanna drive it".

Wheel/tyre sizes

Any 15-inch rim/tyre combination	No problems with rubbing, even extra-low
16 x 7 wheels, 195/45x16 tyres	Also no problems
16 x 7 wheels, 205/40x16 tyres	May catch a little on the arches
16 x 7.5 wheels, 195/45x16 tyres	Slight rubbing problems when car is loaded
17 x 7 or 17 x 7.5 wheels	Rubbing on rear bumper mount, arch lip

We like a challenge

To be honest, successfully fitting big wheels in combination with lowered suspension is one of life's major challenges. As much as anything, tyre width is what ultimately leads to problems, not so much the increased wheel diameter.

If the tyres are simply too wide (or with wheels the wrong offset), they will first of all rub on the suspension strut (ie on the inside edge of the tyre). Also, the inside edges may rub on the arches on full steering lock - check left and right. Rubbing on the inside edges can be cured by fitting offsets or spacers between the wheel and hub, which effectively pull the wheel outwards, 'spacing' it away from its normal position (this also has the effect of widening the car's track, which may improve the on-limit handling - or not). Fitting large offsets must be done using special longer wheel bolts, as the standard ones may only engage by a few threads, which is highly dangerous.

Rubbing on the outside edges is a simple case of wheelarch lip fouling, which must be cured by rolling up (or trimming off) the wheelarch return edge, and other mods. If you've gone for REALLY wide tyres, or have already had to fit offsets, the outer edge of the tyre will probably be visible outside the wheelarch, and this is a no-no (it's illegal, and you must cover it up!). One known Punto problem area is wear in the rear trailing arm bushes - if your Punto is suffering at all, the excess sideways movement will cause your large rims to rub when cornering hard.

On Puntos, it's really the rear arches which cause any great problems, with the rear bumper mounting a particular pain if you're wanting 17s on there. Success may mean removing the bumper (as described in 'Body styling'), doing any necessary trimming, then finding another method of attaching the bumper (we've heard of self-tappers being used for this, but it sounds dicey - at least use mastic in addition).

The other trick with fitting big alloys is of course to avoid the 'Punto 4x4 off-road' look, which you will achieve remarkably easily just by popping on a set of 17s with standard suspension. The massive increase in ground clearance is fine for Farmer Palmer, but your 'fistable' arches won't win much admiration at cruises. Overcoming this problem by lowering can be a matter almost of inspired guesswork, as much as anything (see 'Suspension').

Speedo error? Or not?

One side-effect of fitting large wheels is that your car will go slower. Yes, really - or at least - it will appear to go slower, due to the effects of the mechanically-driven speedometer.

As the wheel diameter increases, so does its circumference (distance around the outside) - this means that, to travel say one mile, a large wheel will turn less than a smaller wheel. Because the speedometer is driven from the gearbox final drive, the apparent vehicle speed is actually based on the number of complete revolutions of the wheel. Therefore, for a given *actual* speed, since a larger-diameter wheel will be turning at a slower rate than a smaller wheel, and the method for measuring speed is the rate of wheel rotation, a car with larger wheels will produce a lower

speedo reading than one with smaller wheels - but it's NOT actually going any slower in reality. So don't worry if you think you've reduced your Punto's performance somehow with the monster rims, 'cos you 'aven't.

With the ever-increasing number of those lovely grey/yellow roadside boxes with a nasty surprise inside, spare a thought to what this speedo error could mean in the real world. If (like most people) you tend to drive a wee bit over the posted 30s and 40s, your real speed on 17s could be a bit more than the bit more you thought you were doing already, and you could get an unexpected flash to ruin your day. What we're saying is, don't drive any faster, to compensate for the lower speedo reading. Actually, the speedo error effect on 17s really is tiny at around-town speeds, and only becomes a factor over 70. But then, Officer, you couldn't possibly have been going over 70, could you? Officer?

Jargon explained

Rolling Radius - You may have come across the term 'rolling radius', which is the distance from the wheel centre to the outer edge of the tyre, or effectively, half the overall diameter. The rolling radius obviously increases with wheel size, but up to a point, the effects are masked by fitting low-profile tyres, with 'shorter' sidewalls. Above 16-inch rims, however, even low-profiles can't compensate, and the rolling radius keeps going up.

PCD - this isn't a banned substance, it's your Pitch Circle Diameter, which relates to the spacing of your wheel holes, or 'bolt pattern'. It is expressed by the diameter of a notional circle which passes through the centre of your wheel bolts, and the number of bolts. Unlike the offset, the PCD often isn't stamped onto the wheels, so assessing it is really a matter of eyeing-up and trying them on the studs - the wheel bolts should go in easily, without binding, if the pattern is correct. On a Punto, the PCD is 98 mm with four studs, which is given as 98/4, or 4 x 98.

Offset - this is determined by the distance from the wheel mounting face in relation to its centre-line. The offset figure is denoted by ET (no, I mustn't), which stands for einpress tiefe in German, or pressed-in depth (now I KNOW you're asleep). The lower the offset, the more the wheels will stick out. Fitting wheels with the wrong offset might bring the wheel into too-close contact with the brake and suspension bits, or with the arches. Very specialised area - seek advice from the wheel manufacturers if you're going for a very radical size (or even if you're not). The correct offset for Puntos of all sizes is ET 40.

Hold on to your wheels

The minute you bang on your wicked alloys, your car becomes a target. People see the big wheels, and automatically assume you've also got a major stereo, seats and other goodies - all very tempting, but that involves breaking in, and you could have an alarm. Pinching the wheels themselves, now that's a doddle - a few tools, some bricks or a couple of well-built mates to lift the car, and it's easy money

The trouble with fitting big wheels is that they're only screwed on, and are just as easily screwed off, if you don't make life difficult for 'em. If you're unlucky enough to have to park outside at night (ie no garage), you could wake up one morning to a car that's *literally* been slammed on the deck! Add to this the fact that your car isn't going anywhere without wheels, plus the damage which will be done to exhaust, fuel and brake pipes from dropping on its belly, and it's suddenly a lot worse than losing a grand's worth of wheels and tyres...

The market and demand for stolen alloys is huge, but since most people don't bother having them security-marked in any way, once a set of wheels disappears, they're almost impossible to trace. Thieves avoid security-marked (or 'tattooed') wheels (or at least it's a pretty good

deterrent) - and it needn't look hideous!

When choosing that car alarm, try and get one with an 'anti-jacking' feature, because thieves hate it. This is sometimes now called 'anti-tilt', to avoid confusion with anti-hijacking. Imagine a metal saucer, with a metal ball sitting on a small magnet in the centre. If the saucer tilts in any direction, the ball rolls off the magnet, and sets off the alarm. Highly sensitive, and death to anyone trying to lift your car up for the purpose of removing the wheels - as we said, the crims are not fond of this feature at all. Simply having an alarm with anti-shock is probably not good enough, because a careful villain will probably be able to work so as not to create a strong enough vibration to trigger it - mind you, it's a whole lot better than nothing, especially if set to maximum sensitivity.

Locking nuts/bolts

Locking wheel bolts will be effective as a deterrent to the inexpert thief (kids, in other words), but will probably only slow down the pro.

Thieves want to work quickly, and will use large amounts of cunning and violence to deprive you of your stuff. If you fit a cheap set of locking bolts, they'll use a hammer and thin chisel to crack off the locking bolt heads. Some bolts can easily be defeated by hammering a socket onto the bolt head, and undoing the locking bolt as normal, while some of the key-operated bolts are so pathetic they can be beaten using a small screwdriver. So - choose the best bolts you can, but don't assume they'll prevent your wheels from disappearing. Insurance companies seem to like 'em - perhaps it shows a responsible attitude, or something...

There's some debate whether it's okay to fit more than one set of locking bolts to a car - some people we know value their wheels so highly, they've fitted four sets of bolts - in other words, they've completely replaced all the standards! The downside is, replacement locking bolts may not be the same quality as factory originals, and while it's okay to fit one set on security grounds, fitting more than that is dangerous on safety grounds (bolt could fail, wheel falls off, car in ditch, owner in hospital...).

Obviously, you must carry the special key or tool which came with your bolts with you at all times, in case of a puncture, or if you're having any other work done, such as new brakes or tyres. The best thing to do is rig this onto your keyring, so it's with you, not left in the car. The number of people who fit locking bolts and then leave the key to them cunningly 'hidden' in the glovebox or the boot... You don't leave a spare set of car keys in your glovebox as well, do you?

How to change a set of wheels

You might think you know all about this, but do you really?

Okay, so you know you need a jack and wheelbrace (or socket and ratchet), but where are the jacking points? If you want to take more than one wheel off at a time, have you got any axle stands, and where do they go? If you've only ever had wheels and tyres fitted by a garage, chances are you're actually a beginner at this. It's surprising just how much damage you can do to your car, and to yourself, if you don't know what you're doing - and the worst thing here is to think you know, when you don't...

What to use

If you don't already have one, invest in a decent hydraulic (trolley) jack. This is way more use than the standard car jack, which is really only for emergencies, and which isn't really stable enough to rely on. Lifting and lowering the car is so much easier with a trolley jack, and you'll even look professional. Trolley jacks have a valve, usually at the rear, which must be fully tightened (using the end of the jack handle) before raising the jack, and which is carefully loosened to lower the car down - if it's opened fully, the car will not so much sink as plummet!

Axle stands are placed under the car, once it's been lifted using the jack. Stands are an important accessory to a trolley jack, because once they're in place, there's no way the car can come down on you - remember that even a brand new trolley jack could creep down (if you haven't tightened the valve), or could even fail completely under load (if it's a cheap one, or knackered, or both).

Under NO circumstances use bricks, wooden blocks or anything else which you have to pile up, to support the car - this is just plain stupid. A Punto may be a small car, but it still weighs quite enough to damage you convincingly if it lands on top of you - if you don't believe us, try crawling under it when it's resting on a few poxy bricks.

Where to use it

Only ever jack the car up on a solid, level surface (ideally, a concrete or tarmac driveway, or quiet car park). If there's even a slight slope, the car's likely to move (maybe even roll away) as the wheels are lifted off the ground. Jacking up on a rough or gravelled surface is not recommended, as the jack could slip at an awkward moment - such as when you've just got underneath...

How to do it - jacking up the front

Before jacking up the front of the car, pull the handbrake on firmly (you can also chock the rear wheels, if you don't trust your handbrake).

If you're taking the wheels off, loosen the wheel bolts before you start jacking up the car. It's easily forgotten, but you'll look pretty silly trying to undo the wheel bolts with the front wheels spinning in mid-air.

We'll assume you've got a trolley jack. The next question is - where to stick it? Up front, there's a hefty subframe behind the engine, with the front suspension wishbones attached - as long as you don't jack under the wishbones, this should be fine, but put a flat offcut of wood on your jack head first, to spread the load. There's also a chunky box-section on the floorpan, running back from the subframe, which can be used for

jacking, again with some wood on the jack head. You can jack on the sill jacking points, which are marked by a triangular-shaped indent, or an arrow, on the sill (there may be a plastic cover to remove first), but it's better to leave those for your axle stands.

Once you've got the car up, pop an axle stand or two under the front sill jacking points - this is the only part of the sill it's safe to jack under or rest the car on. With the stands in place, you can lower the jack so the car's weight rests on the stands. For maximum safety, spread the car's weight between the stands and the jack - don't lower the jack completely unless it's needed elsewhere.

I'm sure we don't need to tell you this, but don't jack up the car, or stick stands under the car, anywhere other than kosher jacking and support points. This means - not the floorpan or the sump (you'll cave it in), not the moveable suspension bits (not stable), and not under the brake/fuel pipes (ohmigawd).

How to do it - jacking up the rear

When jacking up the rear of the car, place wooden chocks in front of the front wheels to stop it rolling forwards, and engage first gear.

If you're taking the wheels off, you don't have to loosen the wheel bolts before lifting the car, but you'll be relying on your handbrake to hold the wheels while you wrestle with the bolts. Much cooler (and safer) to loosen the rear wheel bolts on the ground too.

Jacking and supporting the Punto back-end is a little trickier. Have a good look under there before making your choice. There's a hefty crossmember between the rear wheels which may be used, but watch that no suspension bits are being compressed, and that no pipes or cables get crushed. Otherwise, it's a bit of a minefield - there's the fuel tank, exhaust, brake pipes, anti-roll bar and spare wheel pan to avoid. Not easy.

Fiat's recommended rear jacking point, which you can use to pick up the whole back end, is the central member just inside the bottom lip of the rear bumper. You'll need a really good jack for this, and use a long, sturdy piece of wood to spread the load. There's a rear axle mounting just behind the coil spring, and a strengthened section of floorpan behind that, which you could use, but the block of wood on the jack head's essential equipment here. We used the strengthened section of floorpan just in from the rear sill jacking points, again with some wood to spread the load.

For axle stands, it's the rear sill jacking point, again marked with an indent or arrow on the sill. Not so much need for a block of wood here, but still not a bad idea to use one if you can - saves your paint, spreads the load into the car.

Remember not to put your axle stands under any pipes, the spare wheel well, or the fuel tank, and you should live to see another Christmas.

Finally...

As far as possible, don't leave the car unattended once it has been lifted, particularly if kids are playing nearby - football goes under your car, they go under to get it, knock the jack, car falls... it would almost certainly be your fault.

Changing
wheels

01 Have you got a nice ally/plastic ring inside the wheel hub? Make sure it's there, as it acts to centre the wheel properly, and may help to stop the wheel rusting on. Ever had a rusted-on wheel? Your local fast-fit centre will have, and they'll tell you it ain't funny.

02 Even with the plastic ring of confidence, the metal bits can still corrode on. Equip yourself with some copper brake grease, and smear some on the hub. The pros 'paint' it on with a brush - the rest of us get messy.

03 Now the wheel can go on. Looking good already.

Would be nice if some of that copper grease finds its way onto the threads . . .

04

. . . of the famous 'wobbly bolts'. Don't look much, do they? But if you look closely, you can see that the collar's quite a baggy fit on the bolt, and this is enough to let us fit our 4x100 bolt pattern Momo GT-Rs.

05

Companies like Draper do a set of special sockets with plastic protector sleeves fitted, to stop the metal scratching your fine alloys. Makes sense to us, but - they won't fit on our wheels, with our bolts. Next-best thing? Wrap a little tape round the socket . . .

06

. . . and don't be shy about tightening, for fairly obvious reasons. Still, don't over-tighten, or you'll never get them off if you have a flat! If you've got a torque wrench, you can do them to the proper torque (85 Nm) - if not, do them up as tight as poss with just the wheelbrace in the toolkit (which is all you'll have to undo them with, in an emergency). Smart thinking.

07

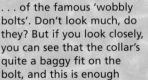
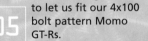

Always nice to see a good brand of tyre on a decent alloy. How cool do cheap tyres look?

Tyres

To some people, tyres are just round and black - oh, and they're nearly all expensive, and don't last long enough. When you're buying a new set of wheels, most centres will quote prices with different tyres - buying a tyred-up set of rims is convenient, and usually good value, too.

Some people try and save money by fitting 'remould' or 're-manufactured' tyres. These aren't always the bargain they appear to be - experience says there's no such thing as a good cheap tyre, with wheel balancing problems a well-known downside, for starters.

Choosing a known brand of tyre will prove to be one of your better decisions. Tyres are the only thing keeping you on the road, as in steering, braking and helping you round corners - what's the point of trying to improve the handling by sorting the suspension if you're going to throw the gains away by fitting naff tyres? Why beef up the brakes if the tyres won't bite? The combination of stiff suspension and cheap tyres is inherently dangerous - because the front end dives less with reduced suspension travel, the front tyres are far more likely to lock and skid under heavy braking.

Cheap tyres also equals more wheelspin - might be fun to disappear in a cloud of tyre smoke, but wouldn't you rather be disappearing up the road? Another problem with really wide tyres is aquaplaning - hit a big puddle at speed, and the tyre skates over the water without gripping - it's seriously scary when your car starts

Tricks 'n' tips
When buying tyres, look out for ones which feature a rubbing strip on the sidewall - these extend over the edge of the wheel rims, and the idea is that they protect the rim edges from damage by 'kerbing'. Any decent tyre has them - discreet and very practical, and much better than a chewed-up rim.

The size markings are obviously the most important, but take note of the directional marks too, if swapping wheels round. Most of the other markings are for anoraks only.

steering for you. Fitting good tyres won't prevent it, but it might increase your chances of staying in control. The sexiest modern low-profile tyres have a V-tread pattern, designed specifically to aid water dispersal, which is exactly what you need to prevent aquaplaning - try some, and feel the difference!

Finally, cheap tyres ruin the look - a no-name brand in big letters on your tyre sidewalls says you're a pikey loud and clear. If you're spending big dosh on wheels, you've gotta kit 'em out with some tasty V-tread tyres, or lose major points for style. Listen to friends and fellow modifiers - real-world opinions count for a lot when choosing tyres (how well do they grip, wet or dry? How many miles can you get out of them?) Just make sure, before you splash your cash on decent tyres, that you've cured any rubbing and scrubbing issues, as nothing will rip your new tyres out faster.

Marks on your sidewalls

Tyre sizes are expressed in a strange mixture of metric and imperial specs - we'll take a typical tyre size as an example:

205/40 R 17 V
for a 7-inch wide 17-inch rim
205 width of tyre in millimetres
40 this is the "aspect ratio" (or "profile") of the tyre, or the sidewall height in relation to tyre width, expressed as a percentage, in this case 40%. So - 40% of 205 mm = 82 mm, or the height of the tyre sidewall from the edge of the locating bead to the top of the tread.
R Radial.
17 Wheel diameter in inches.
V Speed rating (in this case, suitable for use up to 150 mph).

Pressure situation

Don't forget, when you're having your new tyres fitted, to ask what the recommended pressures should be, front and rear - it's unlikely that the Fiat specs for this will be relevant to your new low-low profiles, but it's somewhere to start from. If the grease-monkey fitting your tyres is no help on this point, contact the tyre manufacturer - the big ones might even have a half-useful website. If you're really stuck, try 30 psi all round as a rough guide. Running the tyres at the wrong pressures is particularly stupid (you'll wear them out much faster) and can be very dangerous (too soft - heavy steering, tyre rolls off the rim; too hard - tyre slides, no grip).

Speed ratings

Besides the tyre size, tyres are marked with a maximum speed rating, expressed as a letter code:

T   up to 190 km/h (118 mph)

U   up to 200 km/h (124 mph)

H   up to 210 km/h (130 mph)

V   inside tyre size markings (225/50 VR 16) over 210 km/h (130 mph)

V   outside tyre size markings (185/55 R 15 V) up to 240 km/h (150 mph)

Z   inside tyre size markings (255/40 ZR 17) over 240 km/h (150 mph)

If you've got marks on your sidewalls like this, you're in trouble - this has almost certainly been caused by "kerbing".

08 Suspension

If your Punto is still sitting on standard suspension, it's safe to say it doesn't cut it - yet. If you've decided you couldn't wait to fit your big rims, the chances are your Punto is now doing a passable impression of a tractor. An essential fitment, then - so how low do you go, and what nasty side-effects will a lowering kit have?

The main reason for lowering is of course, to make your car look cool. Standard suspension nearly always seems to be set too soft and too high - a nicely lowered motor really stands out instantly. Lowering your car should also improve the handling. Dropping the car on its suspension brings the car's centre of gravity closer to its roll and pitch centres, which helps to pin it to the road in corners and under braking - combined with stiffer springs and shocks, this reduces body roll and increases the tyre contact patch on the road. BUT - if improving the handling is really important to you, choose your new suspension carefully. If you go the cheap route, or want extreme lowering, then you could end up with a car that don't handle at all...

As for what to buy, there are basically three main options when it comes to lowering, arranged in order of ascending cost below:

1 Set of lowering springs.

2 Matched set of lowering springs and shock absorbers (suspension kit).

3 Set of 'coilovers'.

Lowering springs

The cheapest option by far, but with the most pitfalls and some unpleasant side-effects. Lowering springs are, effectively, shorter versions of the standard items fitted to your Punto at the factory. However, not only are they shorter (lower), they are also uprated (stiffer) - if lowering springs were simply shorter than standard and the same stiffness (the same 'rate'), you'd be hitting the bump-stops over every set of catseyes. With lowering springs, you just fit the new springs and keep the original shock absorbers ('dampers'), so even if the originals aren't completely knackered, you're creating a problem caused by mis-matched components. The original dampers were carefully chosen to work with the original-rate springs - by increasing the spring rate without changing the dampers, you end up with dampers that can't control the springs properly. What this usually does before long is wreck the dampers, so you don't even save money in the end.

The mis-matched springs and dampers will have other entertaining side-effects, too. How would you like a Punto which rides like a brick, and which falls over itself at the first sign of a corner taken above walking pace? A very choppy ride and strange-feeling steering (much lighter, or much heavier, depending on your luck) are well-documented problems associated with taking the cheap option, and it doesn't even take much less time to fit, compared to a proper solution. Even if you're a hard man, who doesn't object to a hard ride if his car looks cool, think on this - how many corners do you know that are completely flat (ie without any bumps)? On dodgy lowering springs, you hit a mid-corner bump at speed, and it's anyone's guess where you'll end up.

If cost is a major consideration, and lowering springs the only option for now, at least try to buy branded items of decent quality - some cheap sets of springs will eat their way through several sets of dampers before you realise the springs themselves have lost the plot. Needless to say, if riding around on mis-matched springs and shocks is a bit iffy anyway, it's downright dangerous when they've worn out (some inside 18 months!).

Assuming you want to slam your suspension so your arches just clear the tops of your wicked new rims, there's another small problem with lowered springs - it takes some inspired guesswork (or hours of careful measuring and head-scratching) to assess the required drop accurately, and avoid that nasty rubbing sound and the smell of burning rubber. Springs are generally only available in a very few sizes, expressed by the amount of drop they'll produce. Punto-wise, a 40 mm drop is a popular choice for retaining good handling, and for not having too many arch-rubbing moments. Much more of a drop is just for the look - a 60 mm drop on 17s is getting pretty hardcore. Take as many measurements as possible, and ask around your mates (or check on 'net forums) - suppliers and manufacturers may be your best source of help in special cases.

Suspension **kit**

A far better choice, Sir - a matched set of springs and dampers is a genuine 'upgrade', and respect is due. There are several branded kits available, and some Fiat specialists do their own. With a properly-sorted conversion, your Punto will handle even better, and you'll still be able to negotiate a set of roadworks without needing dental work afterwards. Actually, you may well be amazed how well the Punto will still ride, even though the springs are clearly lower and stiffer - the secret is in the damping.

Some of the kits are billed as 'adjustable', but this only applies to the damper rates (don't mistake them as being cheap coilovers), which can often be set to your own taste by a few minutes' work. This Playstation feature can be a good fun thing to play around with, even if it is slightly less relevant to road use than for hillclimbs and sprints - but don't get carried away and set it too stiff, or you'll end up with an evil-handling car and a CD player that skips over every white line on the road!

Unfortunately, although you should end up with a fine-handling car, there are problems with suspension kits, too. If you don't have your steering geometry (camber and tracking) reset, you'll eat tyres, and once again, you're into guesswork territory when it comes to assessing your required drop for big wheels. Generally, most suspension kits are only available with a fairly modest drop (typically, 35 to 40 mm).

Coilovers

If you've chosen coilovers, well done again. This is the most expensive option, and it offers one vital feature that the other two can't - true adjustability of ride height, meaning that you can make the finest of tweaks to hunker down on your new rims, or wind it back up when all your mates are on board. Coilovers are a variation on the suspension kit theme - a set of matched variable-rate springs (some have separate 'helper' springs too) and shocks, but their adjustability might not guarantee as good a ride/handling mix as a normal kit.

A coilover set replaces each spring and shock with a combined unit where the coil spring fits over the shocker (hence 'coil' 'over') - nothing too unusual in this, because so far, it's similar to a normal front strut. The difference lies in the adjustable spring lower seat, which can lower the spring (and car) to any desired height, within limits.

Unfortunately, making a car go super-low is not good for the ride or the handling. Coilover systems have very short, stiff springs, and this can lead to similar problems to those found with cheap lowering springs alone. If you go too far with coilovers, you can end up with a choppy ride, heavy steering and generally unpleasant handling. Combine a coilover-slammed car with big alloys, and while the visual effect may be stunning, the driving experience might well be very disappointing. At least a proper coilover kit will come with shock absorbers (dampers) which are matched to the springs, unlike a 'conversion' kit.

Coilover conversion

A better-value option is the 'coilover conversion'. If you really must have the lowest, baddest machine out there, and don't care what the ride will be like, these could be the answer. Offering as much potential for lowering as genuine coilovers (and at far less cost), these items could be described as a cross between coilovers and lowering springs, because the standard dampers are retained (this is one reason why the ride suffers). What you get is a new spring assembly, with adjustable top and bottom mounts - the whole thing slips over your standard damper. Two problems with this solution (how important these are is up to you):

1 Your standard dampers will not be able to cope with the uprated springs, so the car will almost certainly ride (and possibly handle) like a pig if you go for a really serious drop - and okay, why else would you be doing it?

2 The standard dampers are effectively being compressed, the lower you go. There is a limit to how far they will compress before being completely solid (and this could be the limit for your lowering activities). Needless to say, even a partly-compressed damper won't be able to do much actual damping - the results of this could be... interesting...

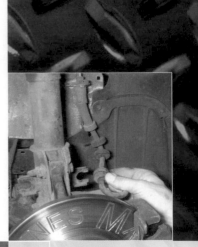

Front Suspension

Tricks 'n' tips

A few days before attacking your suspension, spray some WD-40 on the various mounting nuts and bolts. Shearing off one of the suspension mountings is a great way to ruin your weekend. If any of the nuts/bolts proves really tough to loosen (or goes a little way, then sticks), try tightening it a small amount before getting out the cracker bars - a little movement, even if it's the wrong way, might prevent a fastener from shearing.

Tricks 'n' tips

Don't start this job without coil spring compressors, or you'll be sorry! A torque wrench is also pretty important.

01 Loosen the wheel bolts, jack up the corner of the car you're working on (see Wheels & tyres for more info on jacking), and remove the wheel. First job is to unclip the brake hose from its strut bracket and move the hose to one side - tie it back if necessary. On models with ABS, unclip the wheel sensor wiring too.

02 Next, get in there with the wire brush, and give your nuts a good seeing-to . . .

03 . . . follow this up with a squirt of penetrating spray, and there'll be lots less swearing and skinned knuckles when you come to loosen them off. I know we said Puntos don't rust - these suspension bolts might be the exception.

04 Loosen off the two nuts securing the front strut to the hub, holding the bolt head with another spanner, to stop it turning.

05 Now tap out the two bolts, noting they fit from the front . . .

06 . . . and separate the hub from the strut bracket (again, a small amount of persuasion with a hammer might be needed before things go your way).

07 Back up to the engine bay, and after unclipping a strange plastic ring from the strut top mounting, there's two diagonally-opposite bolts to undo . . .

08 . . . then two plastic pegs are all that's holding the strut up in there. Hold the strut from underneath (mainly to stop it landing on your foot), and release the pegs by squeezing their legs. Poetic, that's what it is.

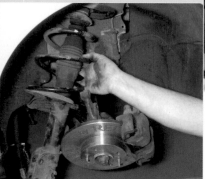

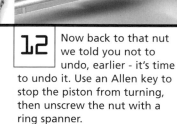

09 The nasty, dirty, generally-unattractive old strut can now be lowered out from the wheel arch, and taken off for surgery.

10 The first item to be removed when our strut hit the workbench was this rubber cap on top, which reveals a rather vital nut underneath. BUT - do not even think about undoing that nut until the spring compressors are in place!

11 Fit the spring compressors to 'grab' as many of the spring coils as you can, and fit them directly opposite each other. Tighten the bolt that runs up the centre of each clamp. Remember to tighten each clamp evenly, or the unclamped side may fly off and cause injury. Compress the spring until the tension is off the strut upper mounting plate.

12 Now back to that nut we told you not to undo, earlier - it's time to undo it. Use an Allen key to stop the piston from turning, then unscrew the nut with a ring spanner.

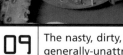

Respect

For the next bit, you MUST use coil spring compressors ('spring clamps'). Medical attention will be required if you don't. Do we have to draw you a diagram? The spring's under tension on the strut, even off the car - what do you think's gonna happen if you just undo it? The spring-embedded-in-the-forehead look is really OVER, too.

13 With the nut removed, it's game on - strut-stripping in progress. Start by removing the top washer . . .

14 . . . then the bush and upper mounting plate (which still contains those plastic pegs). Keep all the old bits from the top of the strut, as we'll be refitting most of them later. Take care when removing the old spring, as it's still under major tension. When removing the spring clamps from the coils, which is the next job, loosen them slowly and evenly, or you'll end up having a very bad day!

15 Take the correct strut for the side of the car you're working on, and prep the piston by pulling it fully out. Then slip the washer (Spax call it a bump stop protector – check to see if your kit has one) onto the piston and fit the bump stop.

16 Now it's time the shiny new spring went on. Use the correct spring, the right way up (if it's not obvious which spring to use, check the markings on the spring, and refer to the kit manufacturer's notes). Even if the springs look the same, they may have different rates (stiffness) so check first.

17 The upper spring seat supplied in our kit is the next part to be added. The new springs are a lot smaller in width than the originals, so this is vital for locating the top of the spring.

18 After the upper spring seat comes this spacer washer . . .

19 . . . followed by a familiar-looking upper mounting plate and bush . . .

20 . . . then the original washer, and a new Nyloc nut. It's important not to mix up the original parts from the left- and right-hand sides. Easiest way to avoid this? Work on one side at a time.

21 The new strut doesn't have an Allen key fitting for the strut piston - instead, you hold it using a smaller spanner than the one needed for the nut. Much easier. Do the nut up as tight as you sensibly can - the torque is 60 Nm, but using a torque wrench on this is pretty-much impossible.

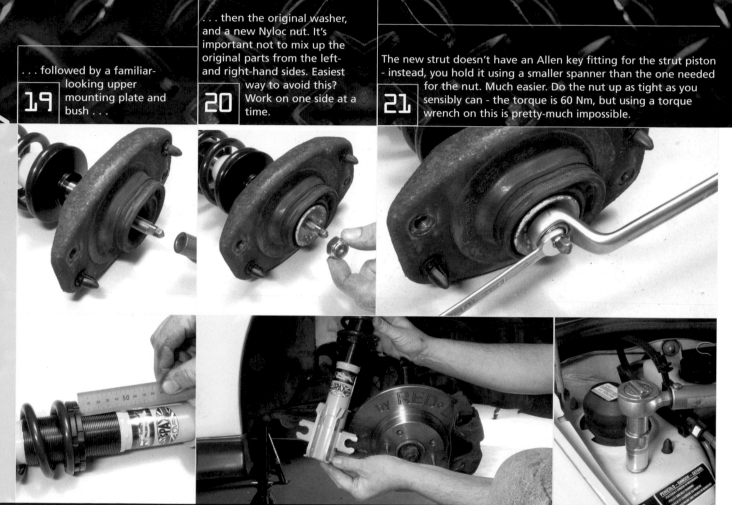

22 If you're fitting coilovers, set the ride height of the springs evenly on both sides (measure with a ruler). You can adjust the height later when the car is back on the ground, keeping it level by simply turning the height adjuster and locking rings the same number of turns each side.

23 The newly-assembled strut can now go back into position in the arch (so nice to have new struts colour-coded to our yellow Punto). Align the upper mounting with the holes in the wing, and push the strut upwards to engage the plastic legs.

24 Refit the strut top mounting bolts, and tighten them securely (or to 50 Nm, if you have the tools for the job).

>>

25 Engage the hub into the mounting bracket on the base of the new strut. Fit the strut-to-hub bolts in from the front, and add the nuts behind, loosely for now. No, these aren't new bolts (though it's not a bad idea to fit new, if your old ones are shot) - we just cleaned ours up with a wire brush.

26 The strut-to-hub nuts/bolts should really be tightened when the car's back on its wheels. To simulate some load being applied, place a jack securely under the base of the hub, and raise it until the suspension starts to compress (don't really lift the car - that might make things a bit unstable for tightening).

27 Tighten the strut-to-hub nuts to 70 Nm, holding the bolts still using a spanner (same as you did for loosening earlier). When both nuts/bolts are tight, you can take away the jack underneath the hub.

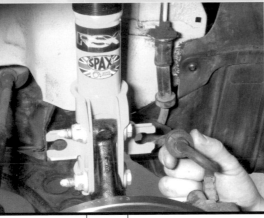

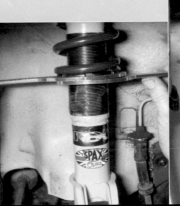

28 Refit the brake hose into its new bracket. If your kit doesn't have a bracket to attach the hose to, you'll be in trouble with the MoT tester – it's a failure to have flapping brake hoses! If this is the case – you will have to engineer yourself a suitable bracket.

29 You can now set the ride height by winding the top ring up or down (height adjustment ring) using the C-spanners supplied, then counter-lock the adjustment ring in position with the lower (locking) ring. A bit of lube applied to the threads will aid future height adjustment.

30 The damper setting for the fronts is critical to how the car drives - it affects the handling/grip, steering feel and braking efficiency. Worth a play then - but don't go too stiff to begin with (your new springs will be stiff enough as it is).

Nasty side-effects

Camber angle and tracking

With any lowering 'solution', it's likely that your suspension and steering geometry will be severely affected - this will be more of a problem the lower you go. This will manifest itself in steering which either becomes lighter or (more usually) heavier, and in tyres which scrub out their inner or outer edges in very short order - not funny, if you're running expensive low-profiles! Sometimes, even the rear tyres can be affected in this way, but that's usually only after some serious slammage. Whenever you've fitted a set of springs (and this applies to all types), have the geometry checked ASAP afterwards.

If you've dropped the car by 60 mm or more, chances are your camber angle will need adjusting. This is one reason why you might find the edges of your fat low-profiles wearing faster than you'd like (the other is your tracking being out). The camber angle is the angle the tyre makes with the road, seen from directly in front. You'll no doubt have seen race cars with the front wheels tilted in at the top, out at the bottom - this is extreme negative camber, and it helps to give more grip and stability in extreme cornering (but if your car was set this extreme, you'd kill the front tyres very quickly!). Virtually all road cars have a touch of negative camber on the front, and it's important when lowering to keep as near to the factory setting as possible, to preserve the proper tyre contact patch on the road. Trouble is, there's not usually much scope for camber adjustment on standard suspension, which is why (for some cars) you can buy camber-adjustable top plates which fit to the strut tops. Setting the camber accurately is a job for a garage with experience of modified cars - so probably not your local fast-fit centre, then.

Rear brake pressure regulator

All Puntos with ABS (and some turbo-diesels) have rear brake pressure-limiting valves fitted, linked to the rear suspension by small springs. The idea is that, when the car's lightly loaded over the rear wheels, the braking effort to the rear is limited, to prevent the wheels locking up. With the boot full of luggage, the back end sinks down, and the valves let full braking pressure through to the rear. When you slam the suspension down, the valves are fooled into thinking the car's loaded up, and you might find the rear brakes locking up unexpectedly - could be a nasty surprise on a wet roundabout! The Punto's valves are not easy to adjust - the best idea would be to crawl underneath and see how they look when unloaded (on standard suspension), and try to re-create the same condition once the car's been dropped.

On the Punto, the brake pressure regulators are under the car, between the rear axle and trailing arm, behind the shock absorber (there's a valve on each side). Chances are, if your Punto's been dropped by much more than 35 to 40 mm, mods will be necessary to make the pressure regulator work properly. The valve attaches to the suspension using a spring - if a slightly longer spring is fitted, when the car's lowered, the valve won't be triggered as soon, so it's one possible answer (though this is a very hit-and-miss approach). If you get major problems with your lowered Punto locking up at the rear under braking, another solution is to disconnect both valve springs completely - this will limit your rear brakes to the pre-lowered level, but won't compensate for when the car's loaded at the rear (so you might have your front brakes locking under heavy braking).

Modifying anything relating to brakes is a very dodgy business - check the results of what you've done very carefully before doing any fast driving. One way to do this is to take the car to an MoT test centre, and have the brakes tested on the rollers. It's no guarantee of faultless brakes under all conditions, but it's better than nothing.

Brace yourself

Another item which is inspired by saloon racing, the strut brace is another underbonnet accessory which you shouldn't be without. Some of them might even work…

The idea of the strut brace is that, once you've stiffened up your front suspension to the max, the car's 'flimsy' body shell (to which the front suspension struts are bolted) may not be able to cope with the 'immense' cornering forces being put through it, and will flex, messing up the handling. The strut brace (in theory) does exactly what it says on the tin, by providing support between the strut tops, taking the load off the bodyshell.

Where this falls down slightly (for road use) is that 1) no-one's going to have the car set that stiff, 2) no-one's going to drive that hard, and 3) the Punto shell isn't exactly made out of tin foil. The strut brace might have a slight effect, but the real reason to fit one is for show - and why not? They look great in a detailed engine bay, and are available in lots of designs and finishes. You're looking at parting with up to a hundred of your finest English pounds, but your mates will be impressed and the girls will love it - and you can't put a price on that!

Rear Suspension

The back end of the car must be raised and supported safely - but you already knew that. To make undoing the shock absorber (damper) lower bolt easier, once the back end's secure on its axle stands, put the jack head under the spring, and raise it a little to just **01** compress the suspension - this takes the load off the bolt.

Lower the jack used to compress the spring. Feed your hand in through the spring coils, and unclip the **02** large plastic disc inside, at the base . . .

07 . . . and the old unit can be lowered away. Don't think we'll be seeing that back on there again.

08 Take one old spring, with rubber mounting pad attached, and un-attach it . . .

09 . . . then transfer the rubber mounting pad (assuming it's not hanging in pieces) to the shiny new spring, making sure it's clipped on properly. There's a fairly obvious end fitting on the rubber pad, which fits onto the end of the new spring. Do the same job on the lower mounting pad . . .

10 . . . and the new spring's ready to offer in place on the car.

03 . . . then use a large screwdriver to prise the bottom of the spring up . . .

04 . . . and off its lower rubber mounting pad (don't damage the rubber - you'll be re-using it) . . .

05 . . . and remove the spring from under the wheel arch.

06 Now the shock absorber top mounting bolt can be removed . . .

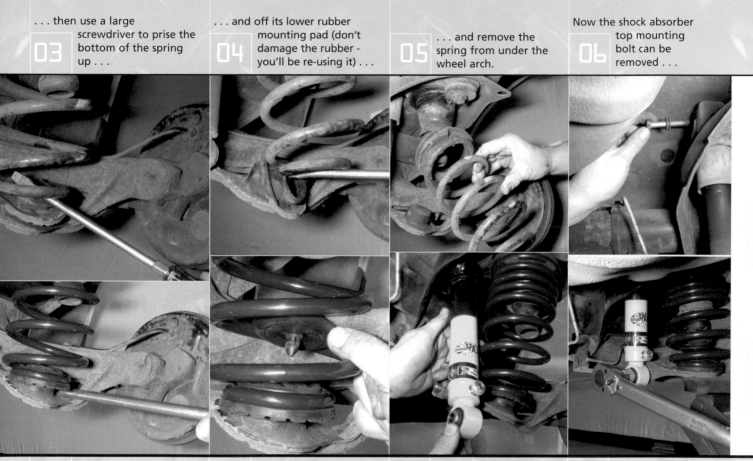

11 Use a suitable lever to help the base of the spring onto the rubber mounting on the suspension arm . . .

12 . . . and don't forget to refit the plastic disc, whose central peg clips into place.

13 Now we're talking - shame no-one's really gonna see this new suspension, 'cos it looks a whole lot more impressive than the old stuff. Offer in the new shock, and slip in the top and bottom mounting bolts. If the bottom bolt won't go in, use a jack under the spring to raise the suspension arm (keep it there, too - you'll need it for tightening the bolt).

14 Use the jack to compress the suspension slightly while the shock bolts are tightened (this simulates the car being back on its wheels). The lower bolt should be torqued to 95 Nm, with the upper one done to 60 Nm. Set your adjustable dampers (not too stiff, and the same both sides), and it's job done.

Brakes

Remember the middle pedal?

It's the one next to the throttle - some people don't use it much. Uprating the brakes is actually a very easy bolt-on upgrade, but there are some points to consider.

One of the strangest, given that improving the brakes should in theory also improve your chances of avoiding an accident, is that insurance companies do not like performance brakes. You should still tell them, but be prepared for bad news. To them, fitting sporty brakes means you drive like Jenson Button - if you need better brakes, you've either also uprated the engine (and not told them?), or you drive on the limit everywhere. Shame. We just like to know our cars will stop quickly. That, actually, might be another reason why they don't like better brakes - you stop better, but does the old dodderer behind you? Crunch.

Uprating the brakes will be a complete waste of time if you're a cheapskate on tyres. Cheap, no-name tyres (or ones with no tread left) won't always be able to translate extra braking power into car-stopping power - they'll give up their grip on the tarmac and skid everywhere. Something like 90% of braking is done by the front wheels - ie the ones you steer with. If you consider that locked-up wheels also don't tend to steer very well, you'll begin to see why top brakes and lame tyres are a well-dodgy mixture.

Groovy discs

Besides the various brands of performance brake pads that go with them, the main brake upgrade is to fit performance front brake discs and pads. Discs are available in two main types - grooved and cross-drilled (and combinations of both).

Grooved discs (which can be had with varying numbers of grooves) serve a dual purpose - the grooves provide a 'channel' to help the heat escape, and they also help to de-glaze the pad surface, cleaning up the pads every time they're used. Some of the discs are made from higher-friction metal than normal discs, too, and the fact that they seriously improve braking performance is well-documented.

Cross-drilled discs offer another route to heat dissipation, but one which can present some problems. Owners report that cross-drilled discs really eat brake pads, more so than the grooved types, but more serious is the fact that some of these discs can crack around the drilled holes, after serious use. The trouble is that the heat 'migrates' to the drilled holes (as was intended), but the heat build-up can be extreme, and the constant heating/cooling cycle can stress the metal to the point where it will crack. Discs which have been damaged in this way are extremely dangerous to drive on, as they could break up completely at any time. Only fit discs of this type from established manufacturers offering a useful guarantee of quality, and check the discs regularly.

Performance discs also have a reputation for warping (nasty vibrations felt through the pedal). Justified, or not? Well, the harder you use your brakes (and we could be talking serious abuse), the greater the heat you'll generate. Okay, so these wicked discs are meant to be able to cope with this heat, but you can't expect miracles. Cheap discs, or ones which have had a mega-hard time over thousands of miles, will warp. So buy quality, and don't get over-heroic on the brakes.

Performance pads can be fitted to any brake discs, including the standard ones, but are of course designed to work best with heat-dissipating discs. Unless your Punto has something seriously meaty under the bonnet, don't be tempted to go much further than 'fast road' pads - anything more competition-orientated may take too long to come up to temperature on the road. Remember what pushbike brakes are like in the wet? Cold competition pads feel the same, and old dears always step off the pavement when your brakes are cold!

Lastly, fitting all the performance brake bits in the world is no use if your calipers have seized up. If, when you strip out your old pads, you find that one pad's worn more than the other, or that both pads have worn more on the left wheel than the right, your caliper pistons are sticking. Sometimes you can free them off by pushing them back into the caliper, but this could be a garage job to fix. If you drive around with sticking calipers, you'll eat pads and discs. You choose.

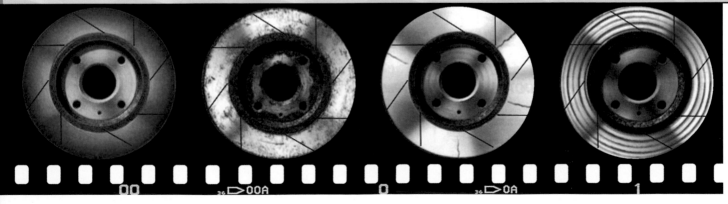

Big disc conversion

Fitting huge multi-spoke wheels makes your factory-fit discs look pretty puny, so many people's idea of impressive brakes is to go large. We can understand that. But it costs, and you might have quite a search to find a company doing the bits, to start with. Then it's got to be decent quality, and fitted properly - if you don't take your brakes seriously, the only mag feature you'll get is Crash of the Month.

Brake discs and pads

01 Loosen the wheel bolts, jack up the corner of the car you're working on, and take off the wheel. Put an axle stand under a suitably-solid part of the car, just in case the jack gives out (see Wheels & tyres). Using a suitable lever, prise the pad retaining spring away from the caliper - note how the clip fits, to make refitting easier.

02 Prise out the protective rubber covers from the two caliper guide bolts . . .

03 . . . then remove the guide pin bolts using the correct-sized Allen key - these bolts may be flippin' tight (make sure you've had your Weetabix).

04 Now the caliper can be lifted away from the disc, together with the inner brake pad (on our Punto) . . .

My calipers don't look like yours

Some Puntos had calipers which are a different design to the ones on our project car. Oops. The best solution to this problem is to buy the Punto Haynes manual, which shows you all you need to know on brakes (plus lots more). However, not wanting to leave you stranded with no hope of sorting your brakes, here's a brief description of how it's done.

At the base of the caliper, you'll see a shiny pin with a small wire clip fitted through it. Pull out the wire clip from the front, then tap out the pin to the inside. Now the caliper body pivots upwards, allowing you access to the two brake pads. When you've changed the pads, tap the pin back in from the inside, and secure by poking the wire clip through the hole. Changing the discs means removing the caliper, which is much the same as on our project car.

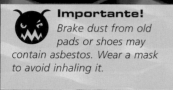

Importante!
Brake dust from old pads or shoes may contain asbestos. Wear a mask to avoid inhaling it.

05 . . . hang the caliper from the spring using wire, string or a cable tie - don't let it hang on the brake hose.

06 Remove the outer brake pad (or both pads) from the caliper carrier. That's very annoying - we're removing pads with plenty of life left. Oh well.

07 Strictly speaking, the caliper carrier doesn't need to come off, to fit new discs. However, like us, you may wish to clean it up in readiness for painting. If so, simply unscrew and remove the upper and lower caliper carrier-to-hub bolts (also very tight), then lift the carrier off.

08 Two small studs are all that's holding the disc on. Doesn't sound very safe, until you remember that the wheel bolts and wheel also clamp the disc to the hub. Undoing these studs should be easy, but remember they'll be rusty - use a quality, close-fitting spanner to avoid rounding them off.

09 At this point you might find the brake disc has rusted itself in place on the hub. Persuade the disc to come away using a hammer - keep hold of the disc, to prevent it suddenly flying off and smacking you in the face! When the disc is free, it can be lifted away from the car.

10 Things are about to get very messy, so put some newspaper down. It's time to clean up the hub, carrier and caliper using plenty of brake cleaner . . .

Remember!
It's a good idea to have your brake mods MOT-tested once you've fitted new discs and pads, and you might even be able to 'blag' a free brake check at your local fast-fit centre if you're crafty! Brakes are a serious safety issue, and unless you're 100% confident that all is well, demo-ing your car's awesome new-found stopping ability could find you in the ditch…

11 . . . lots of wire-brushing, taking care not to damage the dust seal around the piston . . .

12 . . . and finally, some sandpaper. Try not to breathe any of the dust in, as it could be harmful. Worse than smoking, even. Cleaning all rust off the hub is vital, otherwise your new discs may not sit on square, which (at best) will chew through your new pads very fast.

13 Using a suitable solvent (brake cleaner is a good one) remove the oily, sticky, corrosion-preventing film from the discs.

14 Pop the discs into place onto the now-clean, flat hub, and secure with the two disc locating studs. The discs must be fitted the right way round - easy to judge on our engraved discs from Red Dot. On grooved discs, the grooves must face the right way, or they won't be as effective - check your kit's instructions.

15 If you removed it, refit the caliper carrier bracket - torque the two bolts to 53 Nm.

16 Pop the new outer brake pad into position on the carrier.

Remember!
New pads of any sort need careful bedding-in (over 100 miles of normal use) before they'll work properly - when first fitted, the pad surface won't have worn exactly to the contours of the disc, so it won't actually be touching it, over its full area. This will possibly result in very under-whelming brakes for the first few trips, so watch it - misplaced over-confidence in new brakes is a fast track to hospital...

17 If your Punto's like ours, go back to the caliper (still hanging off the spring) and unclip the inner brake pad.

18 Go to the engine bay next, and open the cap on the brake fluid reservoir. If the reservoir is very full, you may need to syphon off some excess fluid - when you push the caliper piston back, the fluid level will rise.

19 The caliper piston now needs to be pushed very slowly back into the caliper, using a G-clamp or proper piston retractor tool, to make room for the new, thicker, brake pads. Keep half an eye on the level in the brake reservoir - if needs be, have some cloth standing by to capture any spillage/overflow.

20 Apply some copper grease to the back of the pad (the side that doesn't contact the disc), and either clip the pad into the caliper, or slide the new brake pad into place on the bracket.

21 Apply some more copper grease to the outer surface of the outer pad, taking great care not to get any grease on the contact area of the pad or the disc.

22 Refit the caliper, remembering to torque the guide pin bolts to the correct figure. In our case, it's 27 Nm, but see your Haynes Manual.

23 Refit the rubber guide pin covers and the pad retaining clip. All that's left now is to refit the wheel and lower the car down.

Brakes

Cool coloured stoppers

One 'downside' to fitting massive multi-spoked alloys is that - gasp - people can see your brakes! So don't be shy about it - paint some of the brake bits so they look the biz, to match (or clash completely) with your chosen colour scheme. Red is the colour inspired by the racing/touring-car boys, but isn't the only choice.

Many Puntos don't have rear discs, but painting the brake drums is acceptable under the circumstances - but then, do you paint 'em black, to de-emphasise them, or in your chosen colour for the fronts? It's all tough decisions, in modifying. If you're really sad, you can always buy fake rear discs… For the less-sad among you, it is possible to convert any Punto to rear discs, by fitting GT rear suspension arms - pricey, but maybe necessary if there's a tuned GT engine going in soon. A rear disc conversion's going a bit far, just to have red calipers front and rear - and remember, the rear brakes don't do much actual stopping…

Painting the calipers requires that they're clean - really clean. Accessory stores sell aerosol brake cleaner, which (apart from having a distinctive high-octane perfume) is just great for removing brake dust, and lots more besides! Some kits come complete with cleaner spray. Many of the kits advertise themselves on the strength of no dismantling being required, but we don't agree. Also, having always successfully brush-painted our calipers, we wouldn't advise using any kind of spray paint.

We know you won't want to hear this, but the best way to paint the calipers is to do some dismantling first. The kits say you don't have to, but trust me - you'll get a much better result from a few minutes' extra work. The best time to paint would be while you're fitting new discs, but nobody thinks that far ahead.

Painting calipers

 01 Thorough preparation will ensure the best paint job on your caliper, so give it a good wire-brush to loosen any dust and rust (inhaling black brake dust not advisable). If your brush is as hardcore as ours, don't go damaging the rubber brake hose, piston seals, or the brake pads (if, unlike us, you haven't stripped the brakes for painting).

02 Use aerosol brake cleaner to wash the worst of the stuff out, particularly in any corners the wire brush couldn't reach. Finally, wipe the caliper over with a cloth, which should get the last of the muck off, to give you a smooth surface - don't rely on spraying alone. Leave it to dry for a few minutes.

03 While the caliper's drying, mask up any bits you don't want to paint - like the bleed screw, caliper mounting bolts, and the rubber brake hose, for instance.

04 Caliper paint has to be the right stuff, otherwise it won't last. We chose MHW's special caliper paint, which comes in a two-part pack, giving you a spray can of cleaner and a tin of paint. Get painting, using a small brush, as it helps for all the difficult-to-reach areas. Don't paint it on too thick, or it'll run.

Painting drums

 01 Now get the rear end jacked up, wheels off (see 'Wheels & tyres' if you need jacking info) and get stuck into the brake drums with the wire brush, then sandpaper (to smooth the surface) . . .

02 . . . spray on the brake cleaner, and wipe thoroughly. Wiping is important - don't rely on the spray alone, as you won't get the surfaces clean.

03 You definitely don't want any paint down the wheel bolt holes - in fact, you don't really want it where the wheels will touch the drum (you can't see this bit, once the wheel's on). You also don't want paint on the drum securing studs, or the brake backplate. Masking-up is the answer.

04 Painting the drums is much easier than the fiddly calipers, but use a decent brush with soft bristles. For a max-shine finish, you need to be generous with the paint, and smooth with your stroke (oh, baby). Let off the handbrake and turn the drum half a turn every so often until the paint's dry. Nobody likes the runs, after all.

interiors

The Punto dash is best described as functional. It does the job, and that's about it. It might have no style whatsoever, but at least it doesn't feel like it's about to fall apart, or come off in your hands, unlike certain popular French superminis we could mention. Yes, the Punto interior (with the exception of some really awfully-nice seat fabrics - not) is pretty dull. But you need suffer no longer, because the interior really is one area where most of the goodies are pretty easy to fit, and provided you go for one particular 'theme' (rather than a mixture), the end result can certainly help you forget you're in a poverty model, if indeed you are...

To be fair to the Punto, not many standard interiors are anything to shout about, particularly when you compare them with the sort of look that can easily be achieved with the huge range of product that's out there. As with the exterior styling, though, remember that fashions can change very quickly - so don't be afraid to experiment with a look you really like, because chances are, it'll be the next big thing anyway. Just don't do wood, ok? We've a feeling it's never coming in, never mind coming back…

Removing stuff

Take it easy and break less

Many of the procedures we're going to show involve removing interior trim panels (either for colouring or to fit other stuff), and this can be tricky. It's far too easy to break plastic trim, especially once it's had a chance to go a bit brittle with age. Another 'problem' with the Punto is that the interior trim is pretty well-attached (and the designers have been very clever at hiding several vital screws), meaning that it can be a pig to get off. We'll try to avoid the immortal words 'simply unclip the panel', and instead show you how properly, but inevitably at some stage, a piece of trim won't 'simply' anything.

The important lesson here is not to lose your temper, as this has a highly-destructive effect on plastic components, and may result in a panel which no amount of carbon film or colour spray can put right, or make fit again. Superglue may help, but not every time. So - take it steady, prise carefully, and think logically about how and where a plastic panel would have to be attached, to stay on. You'll encounter all sorts of trim clips (some more fragile than others) in your travels - when these break, as they usually do, many of them can be bought in packs from accessory shops, and rarer ones will be available from a Fiat dealer, probably off the shelf. Even fully-trained Fiat mechanics aren't immune to breaking a few trim clips!

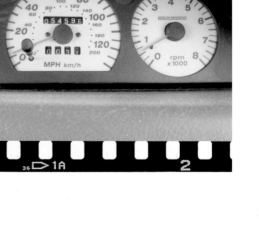

Door trim panel

You'll find plenty of excuses for removing your door trim panels - fitting extra speakers, re-trimming the panel, de-locking, even window tinting, so we'd better tell you how ...

01 Start by prising away the mirror trim panel. Okay - this is easier for us now, as we've fitted some Cup mirrors, which do away with the mirror adjustment knobs (see 'Body styling').

02 Next, remove the screw and work the interior lock handle surround off the handle.

03 Prise the electric window switch from the armrest and disconnect the wiring plug.

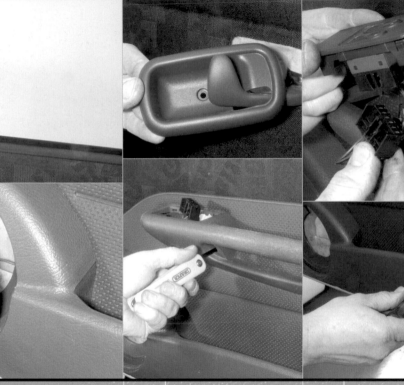

04 Keep prising away - the next thing to remove is the speaker cover and unscrew the actual speaker cone itself (see the ICE section for details), remembering to disconnect its wiring plug.

05 Now there's a mixture of Allen and cross-head screws holding the panel on - some hidden in the door pull ...

06 ... some hidden behind plastic trim caps ...

07 . . . and some hiding round the door edges.

08 Insert a suitable prising tool (something wider than your typical screwdriver) between the door and trim panel to release the press-stud clips keeping the panel in place.

09 You're now ready to lift the panel upwards, over the door lock knob and away from the car.

10 Should you wish to gain access to components inside the door, simply pull back the plastic membrane. Try not to tear it - if it wasn't important, Fiat wouldn't fit it.

Wind-up windows? No worries

For those of you without the benefit of electric motors for your window winding operations, here's how to take off those luvverly plastic handles. The little beggars are held on by a spring clip, which has two small 'legs' sticking out at the bottom. Work the edge of a piece of (clean) cloth/rag into the gap between the handle and the plastic disc, from underneath. Using a 'sawing' action, work the cloth side to side - this catches on the legs, and releases the clip. Takes a while, but it does work - just watch where the spring clip goes!

Anything but black?

The interior trim on the Punto at least hides its age well, and doesn't rattle much. And that's about it - for a lover of elephant-hide grey, it's heaven. For normal people, it's something else. Fortunately, there's plenty you can do to personalise it, and there are three main routes to take:

1) Spray paint - available in any colour you like, as long as it's… not black. This Folia Tec stuff actually dyes softer plastics and leather, and comes in a multi-stage treatment, to suit all plastic types. Don't try to save money just buying the top coat, because it won't work! Special harder-wearing spray is required for use on steering wheels. Ordinary spray paint for bodywork might damage some plastics, and won't be elastic - good primer is essential. Make sure you also buy lots of masking tape.

2) Adhesive or shrink-fit film - available in various wild colours, carbon, ally, and, er… walnut (would YOU?). Probably best used on flatter surfaces, or at least those without complex curves, or you'll have to cut and join - spray is arguably better here. Some companies will sell you sheets of genuine carbon-fibre, with peel-off backing - looks and feels the part (nice if you have touchy-feely passengers).

3) Replacement panels - the easiest option, as the panels are supplied pre-cut, ready to fit. Of course, you're limited then to styling just the panels supplied.

If you fancy something more posh, how about trimming your interior bits in leather? Very saucy. Available in various colours, and hardly any dearer than film, you also get that slight 'ruffled' effect on tighter curves.

Get the cans out

Any painting process is a *multi-stage* application. With the Folia Tec system (thanks to Eurostyling for supplying ours), many of you apparently think you can get away just buying the top coat, which then looks like a cheap option compared to film - WRONG! Even the proper interior spray top coat won't stay on for long without the matching primer, and the finish won't be wear-resistant without the finishing sealer spray. You don't need the special foaming cleaner - you could get by with a general-purpose degreaser, such as meths. Just watch the grey/black plastic doesn't suddenly turn white - if it does, you're damaging the finish! This might not be too important to you, as it's being sprayed over anyway, but if you take out the grey too far on a part that's not being sprayed all over, you'll have to live with a cacky-looking white-grey finish to any non-painted surface...

Providing you're a dab hand with the masking tape, paint gives you the flexibility to be more creative. For instance, you could try colour-matching the exterior of the car - but will ordinary car body paint work on interior plastics? Course it will, as long as you prep the panels properly.

Choice of paint's one thing, but what to paint? Well, not everything - for instance, you might want to avoid high-wear areas like door handles. Just makes for an easier life. The glovebox lid and instrument panel surround are obvious first choices, as are the ashtray and fusebox lid. The centre console's not lighting anyone's fire in standard Fiat grey, so hit it with some spray too. Any panels which just pop out are targets, in fact (lots less masking needed) - just make sure whatever you're dismantling was meant to come apart, or it'll be out with the superglue instead of the cans.

Don't be afraid to experiment with a combination of styles - as long as you're confident you can blend it all together, anything goes! Mix the painted bits with some tasteful carbon-fibre sheet or brushed-aluminium film, if you like - neutral colours like this, or chrome, can be used to give a lift to dash bits which are too tricky to spray.

Painting **trim**

Interiors

01 Place your chosen item of interior trim on a clean, flat surface, and attack with sandpaper. Our aim is to remove the nasty injection-moulded design that looks like elephant hide. Nice. In order to save total disintegration of your hands, it's best to wear gloves (well, you try telling our mechanic).

02 When you're satisfied that enough of the grain pattern has been removed by sandpaper (remember that you carry on the smoothing process by priming the area, rubbing the primer back and repeating the process), clean the area with a suitable degreaser. Try 'panel-wipe' from a bodyshop.

04 Plaster the surrounding area with newspaper (to avoid parental unrest), then add your first layer of plastic primer and leave to dry as per instructions on the can.

05 Rub the primer back with fine-grain sandpaper. Do not rub the primer off; we're aiming partly to fill any gaps left from the elephant hide by building up layers of primer.

06 Repeat this process of building up the primer until the surface is totally smooth. Ours took three layers until we were happy that all elephant hide had been eliminated. It's time to paint. We've chosen to paint our box that same colour as the car, but the possibilities are endless. One coat of paint should be enough – but use two coats if you feel it needs it. End by adding a nice layer of lacquer to make it really shiny!

Filming your **Punto**

If you fancy creating a look that's a bit more special than plain paint colours, film is the answer - but be warned - it's not the easiest stuff in the world to use, and so isn't everyone's favourite. If you must have the brushed-aluminium look, or fancy giving your Punto the carbon-fibre treatment, there really is no alternative (apart from the lazy-man option of new panels, of course).

01 When we made up a switch panel out of some alloy plate for our Punto's centre console, leaving the alloy bare wasn't an option for our interior's yellow and black style. Carbon fibre film to the rescue! Lay the plate in position, and mark round . . .

02 . . . then trim out the shape, remembering to leave some round the edges, for folding over.

03 It's always a good idea to clean up whatever you're sticking film to. On a plastic dash piece, the plastic could have been treated with silicone-based dash spray sometime in its life - clean this off if you ever want anything to stick (remembering that some solvents might attack the plastic finish). Our metal plate's easier to deal with - just rough it up with a little Scotchbrite.

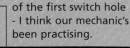

Stick the film on straight - very important with any patterned finish. Start at one edge or corner, and work across, to keep the air bubbles and creases to a minimum. If you get a really bad crease, it's best to unpeel a bit and try again - **04** the adhesive's very tacky, and there's no slide-age available.

Work out the worst of the air bubbles with a soft cloth, or even an old store/credit card (if you're rich). Before doing any trimming or folding, the most important thing is to warm the **05** film - this makes it much easier to work with.

Fold the film around your chosen object, trying to get a perfect crease first time (the more you mess about with it, the less it'll want to **06** stick). Press it into place like you mean it.

Trimming this film requires a sharp knife (a blunt one will tear or ripple the film), and a steady hand (so you don't cut yourself with that sharp knife?). That's a very neat job **07** of the first switch hole - I think our mechanic's been practising.

Bum notes

There are limitations to using film, and the quality of the film itself has a lot to do with that. We had major problems doing any kind of job with one particular make of brushed-aluminium-look film - it was a nightmare to work with, and the edges had peeled the next day. Buying quality film will give you a long-lasting result to be proud of, with much less skill requirement and lots less swearing. But it still pays not to be too ambitious with it.

Dash Dynamics

A far easier route to the brushed-ally or carbon look, pre-finished ('here's some we did earlier') panels are available from suppliers. Dash kits are available for the Mk 1 Punto from companies like Dash Dynamics, and offer a simpler way of livening-up the dull Punto dash.

01 Your first job is to thoroughly clean and degrease the area to which the dash kit is being fitted. Cleaning solution is provided in the kit, and will remove any traces of polish, grease or silicone, so that the glue will work properly and hold the kit in place.

02 Taking care not to touch the area you've just cleaned, raise the temperature of the surface of the dash using a hot-air gun or hairdryer set to a low heat. This enables the glue on the back of each piece of the kit to start the adhesion process faster. We said warm it up - don't melt the dash, or burn yourself!

03 Fit one piece of the kit at a time, begin by applying the same low heat to a section, then peeling off the backing paper. Don't touch the adhesive on the back.

04 Place the section of kit into position on the dash (each section is labelled to show you where it has to be fitted). At this stage, if you're not happy with the position, you can still peel off the kit and reposition it.

05 When you're satisfied everything's properly aligned (on carbon fibre, the weave pattern mustn't be wonky), take a piece of cloth and firmly press down the kit, paying particular attention to the corners and edges of each section.

06 At this stage, add a little more heat to aid the first stages of adhesion. It will take 24 hours for each piece to be fully bonded into place. Over time, you may find the kit may lift in certain areas - if this happens, simply apply some strong adhesive to the area to re-stick it.

Handbrake
knobs & gaiters

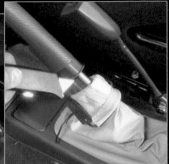

01 Changing the handbrake gaiter is really easy - for a start, the old gaiter just prises out of the centre console, and can be slid off over the handle. Once away from the car, begin by cutting the old gaiter off the plastic frame.

02 The new gaiter should fit over the old frame, but as with our gear gaiter, we had to trim off the elastic base to let it stretch far enough. Be gentle with it once you've done this, as there's a danger of the gaiter's side stitching coming apart if you pull it about. We used our trusty hot glue gun to stick the gaiter snugly in position.

03 Now it's just a case of popping your new gaiter back into position on the console. Push down on it quite hard to make sure it locates correctly - this isn't easy, as the new leather gaiter's thicker than the old one, and may pop up a few times until you've it located in the hole properly.

04 Now to the handbrake handle. The only way of getting that grotty thing off is to cut it off using a sharp blade. It may take some time to hack through the thick plastic of the handle.

Once the handle has been removed, you may find that the return spring on the handbrake has fallen out of place. It is vitally important that the spring is located properly, or the handbrake won't work too well . . . **05**

. . . to make doubly sure that spring won't move around whilst you fit a new handle, tape it up. Better safe than sorry – especially if you park on a hill! **06**

Our sexy new Momo handle is then put into place. As usual, being a quality piece of kit, it fits perfectly. **07**

Tighten the grub screws (supplied within the kit) to hold the handle in place permanently. Last job is to pull the gaiter up to the base of the handle, and tie its laces for it. **08**

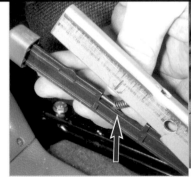
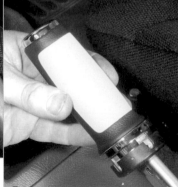

Gear knob jobs

Gear knobs and gaiters are a fairly inexpensive way of modifying the interior look of your car. You spend a lot of time in contact with that knob, so why not treat it to a new look?

01 The first job when changing your gear knob and gaiter is to try and get that awful existing knob off. This is a nightmare. We started trying to cut the knob off using a blade, but ended up using a mini hacksaw.

02 When the soft rubber gear knob cover has been removed, you can understand why this was a beast. The centre part of the gear knob is made up of extremely tough plastic. This hard-as-nails black plastic knob must also be removed so carry on and hacksaw that off as well. Watch out - the plastic will be extremely hot after all your sawing efforts.

03 With that bloomin' knob out the way, you can prise the gaiter out of the console and lift it over the gear lever.

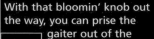

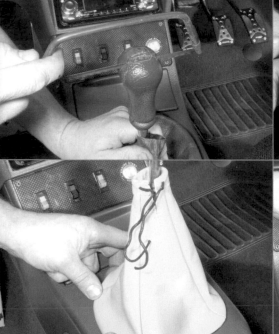

08 Now the new gaiter can be fitted back into the console and pushed firmly down to secure it in place. Looks heaps better already.

09 The collar is the first part of the new Momo gear knob assembly to be slid down the gear lever into place.

10 Next thing to slide over the lever is the correct-sized sleeve – there will be a few different-sized ones supplied in the pack, so try them out to see which one fits best.

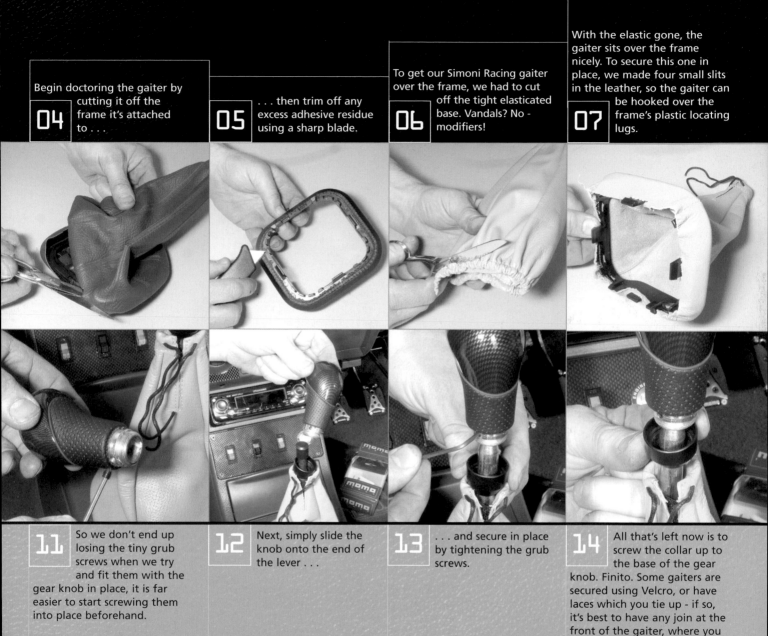

04 Begin doctoring the gaiter by cutting it off the frame it's attached to . . .

05 . . . then trim off any excess adhesive residue using a sharp blade.

06 To get our Simoni Racing gaiter over the frame, we had to cut off the tight elasticated base. Vandals? No - modifiers!

07 With the elastic gone, the gaiter sits over the frame nicely. To secure this one in place, we made four small slits in the leather, so the gaiter can be hooked over the frame's plastic locating lugs.

11 So we don't end up losing the tiny grub screws when we try and fit them with the gear knob in place, it is far easier to start screwing them into place beforehand.

12 Next, simply slide the knob onto the end of the lever . . .

13 . . . and secure in place by tightening the grub screws.

14 All that's left now is to screw the collar up to the base of the gear knob. Finito. Some gaiters are secured using Velcro, or have laces which you tie up - if so, it's best to have any join at the front of the gaiter, where you won't see it.

Under neon light

So how much of a poser are you? How'd you like to show off all this shiny chequer floor and sexy pedals to full effect, in the midnight hour? You need some neons, baby! Yeah!

Bum notes
It appears that interior neons have recently been declared ILLEGAL, and this means, in the first place, you're unlikely to find anywhere that even sells them any more. Exterior neons have been illegal from day one. If you fit interior neons, make sure they're at least easily switched off, should you get pulled. Remember that driving at night with a brightly-lit interior makes it even harder to see out. Neons are best used for show purposes.

01 There's not a great deal to this, really - decide where you want 'em, where you're going to get a live and an earth (and a switch, if necessary), then fit 'em. We wanted our neons up under the dash, to light up the footwells. The first thing to do is offer one in place - remember, it would be sort-of useful if your feet don't hit them as you work the pedals...

02 To mount the tubes, you can use the plastic securing clips supplied with the kit. Mark the holes for drilling . . .

03 . . . and get stuck in there with the cordless. Try not to drill through anything vital, like wiring.

04 We removed the glovebox to make the photo clearer - you can just open it to find the holes you have just drilled. With the tube held in place, pop your screw into the hole and through the hole in the bracket. A nut can be added from below to hold it all in place, and the excess screw threads can be cut off if you wish. Repeat the process for the opposite footwell.

05 Last job is to sort out the wiring. Each tube has a red and a black wire, joined together, so first separate the two. Take the pair of reds, join together in one spade connector, and run it to the switch middle terminal. Our switch is going in the panel we made for our washer jet lights (see 'Body styling'). Take another piece of red wire, and join to the bottom pin on the switch . . .

06 . . . and the other end goes to a live feed. You could go straight to the battery, or get the test light out and find a suitable live in the fusebox. What did we do? Went straight to the auxiliary fusebox we made earlier (see 'Security'), and tapped in there. So easy.

07 To finish off, the two earth wires from the neons are joined together in a ring terminal, and routed to a suitable earth point. By chance, there happened to be one right next to where we mounted our auxiliary fusebox. Time to give your Punto that nightclub feel, without the bouncers.

The personal touch –
re-trimming

Okay, so you're definitely not happy with how the inside of your Punto looks, but you're not sold on any of the off-the-shelf options for tricking it up, either. You know how you want it to look, though, so get creative!

There are any number of upholstery companies in Yellow Pages, who will be able to create any look you want (we got one in our own back yard, almost - Pipers of Sparkford, Somerset, and very helpful lads they are, too). If your idea of Punto heaven is an interior swathed in black and purple leather, these guys can help. Don't assume that you'll have to go to Carisma, to get a car interior re-trimmed - they might well be the daddies at this, but any upholsterer worth the name should be able to help, even if they normally only do sofas!

Of course, if you're even slightly handy with things like glue and scissors, you might be inspired to get brave and DIY. An upholsterers will still be a useful source for materials (and maybe advice too?).

Are your dials
all white?

White dial kits aren't that difficult to fit, but you will need some skill and patience not to damage the delicate bits inside your instrument panel - the risk is definitely worth it, to liven up that dreary grey Punto dash, anyway.

Just make sure you get the right kit for your car, and don't start stripping anything until you're SURE it's the right one - look carefully. Most dial kit makers, for instance, want to know exactly what markings you have on your speedo and rev counter. If they don't ask, be worried - the kit they send could well be wrong for your car, and might not even fit. When you receive your kit, before you even open the packet, ensure that the dials in the kit are an exact match of those in your car.

Safety and electrics go arm in arm, so begin by disconnecting the battery. Check your radio codes before you do, though – we don't want any tears when your stereo doesn't work! Next you need to get to those clocks, so armed with an Allen key, remove the two securing screws from the instrument panel surround.

 01

Carefully pull the panel away from the facia, to reveal four wiring plugs that need to be disconnected next.

 02

Take care when disconnecting the plugs, and to aid refitting, label each plug and its connection point. Once everything has been disconnected, the instrument cluster is now free to be removed from the car and taken to a clean, flat surface to proceed with the next stage of fitting the new dials.

03

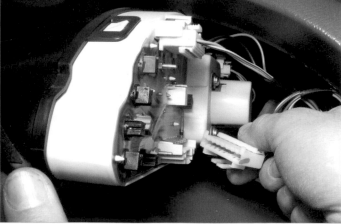

>>

04 Remove the trip meter reset knob by gently pulling it away from its hole in the dial face. Before you go much further, find yourself a clean, shallow dish to hold small, but important, things like this.

05 The first stage of dismantling the cluster is to remove the clear 'lens' and cowl by carefully prising the tabs that can be found on the top and base of the unit . . .

06 . . . then the lens is free to be removed and put in a safe place (damage it while it's off, and you will not be a very happy bunny).

07 Unclip the black dial mask and remove. Carefully.

12 Before you can even think about fitting the new dials, give the backplate a good clean. Use something that will remove glue - we use methylated spirit for jobs like this, and it works a treat.

13 With the kit, you'll find a packet of black 'banjo' shaped washers. There are two sizes – the smaller ones are for the fuel and temperature gauges. These shapes fit round the hub of each needle, and prevent light shining past. Peel off the backing paper to reveal the adhesive, then open the slit in the washer and slide it around the spindle of the needle.

14 Position the washer centrally, making sure the movement of the needle isn't hindered in any way. When you're satisfied with the position, press the banjo firmly into place and cut off the handle. Repeat the process for the remaining three gauges.

15 Now you can start fitting the new dials. Start by taking one of the dials and removing the backing paper to reveal the adhesive.

08 Have that small-parts-holding dish ready - we're about to remove the needle rest pegs (there are four in total, at least on a Sporting). Once the rests have been removed, don't play with the needles - just let them come to their natural resting place, and then leave them alone.

09 Now comes the fun part. Using a sharp knife, cut a slot from the hole through which the spindle of the needle comes, to the edge of the dial. Then cut another slot on the opposite side of the hole, to the other edge of the dial. What a vandal.

10 The face of each gauge (or what's left of it) should now be easy to remove.

11 Repeat this process for the fuel and temperature gauges. Before attempting to remove the speedo face, remove the two screws that secure it to the backplate (don't lose them), then proceed as before.

Very gently move the needle of the gauge you're fitting to the 12 o'clock position, and fit the dial so that the needle enters the hole (let the needle come a natural rest afterwards). When fitting the speedo dial, you have to hook it over the trip meter knob as well as getting the needle through the hole. When you're happy with the position of the dial, press firmly into place.

16

With all the dials done, the speedo retaining screws and all needle rest pegs can be refitted.

17

The dials can then be pressed down once more before refitting the lens cover, just to help the glue do its job.

18

Finally then, give the lens cover a clean, especially the inside (you may have got fingerprints on it, which will really bug you when you refit the cluster to the car). Then refit to the car, retracing your steps for removal.

19

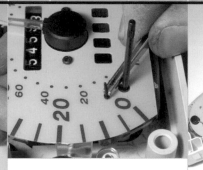
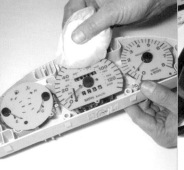

Rev counter

Those of you who already have a rev counter (or tacho), ignore this bit. Or perhaps not - you might want a tidy little tacho mounted somewhere more helpful than in the instrument podule. If so, we're here to help, with this very trick rev counter and carbon fibre windscreen pillar pod.

01 The first job is to decide where you'd like it, and there's all sorts of positions for you to try (are we still talking about a tacho?). We've gone for the popular A-pillar choice for maximum race looks. If you look carefully, you'll see our pod isn't really shaped to fit our A-pillar, so . . .

02 . . . we're using this cunning little gadget, called a profile gauge. By holding it up to the spot we've marked for our pod, and pressing it in place, the exact shape of the curve on the A-pillar is reproduced.

03 Now hold the profile gauge up to the pod, and you can mark it with confidence . . .

04 . . . for accurate trimming. You want a tidy result? This is the way to get it - finish off by smoothing the edge with a file or sandpaper.

05 The A-pillar trim panel should really come off, to make final fitting easier. Luckily, it's just one screw at the top . . .

06 . . . then peel back the door rubber seal, and unclip the trim.

07 At last - the first sighting of our new tacho. Why are we looking at the back, exactly? There's a switch on the back, which lets you set the tacho for different numbers of cylinders. We haven't heard of anyone doing a Punto V6 or V8 conversion, so we'll take a wild guess it's the 4-cylinder position you want.

Tips 'n' tricks
All Puntos have static, distributorless, 'wasted-spark', coil-pack ignition - make sure you only buy a tacho suitable for such a system, or it won't read right.

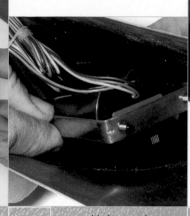

08 At least our new pod didn't need trimming for the gauge to fit like a glove . . .

09 . . . and it locates in there using this bracket behind . . .

10 . . . held on by a couple of nuts.

11 Okay, the new pod's about ready to be mated up to the A-pillar trim we took off earlier. Notice we've already drilled a hole in the panel, so the gauge wiring can go through . . .

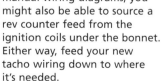
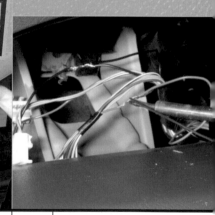

12 . . . now we're drilling four smaller ones, to pass through some cable-ties, which we're using to mount the pod (we don't completely trust the double-sided tape supplied).

13 Pull the wiring through, then fasten the pod with cable-ties, pulled tight and trimmed off. Might not be what it says in the instructions, but we don't care - it's on there, and it looks good.

14 It shouldn't be a great surprise that your clocks have to come out for wiring-up (see the section on white dials for a how-to). Using your Haynes manual wiring diagrams, you might also be able to source a rev counter feed from the ignition coils under the bonnet. Either way, feed your new tacho wiring down to where it's needed.

15 The instrument wiring plugs provide all our wiring feeds, and a little stripping and soldering later, we have a working gauge. New tacho's green wire is the rev signal wire, and joins to our Punto's blue one. The new red wire's for ignition live (to pink), the orange is gauge lighting (to yellow/black), and the black's an earth (to black). Re-sult!

Racing
starts

Like to have a racing-style starter button on your Punto? Read on! A very cool piece of kit, and a great way to impress your passengers.

The idea of the racing starter button is the ignition key's made redundant, beyond switching on the ignition lights (it'd be a bit daft, security-wise, if you could start the engine without the key at all).

The best (and easiest) part is deciding where the button's going. Somewhere highly-visible, obviously (to impress). We're sorted - it's going in the switch panel we made for our washer jet lights (see 'Body styling'). Meanwhile, we need to get into the wiring, which means getting to the ignition switch. Take out three Allen

01 screws, and lower out the steering column shroud.

Before we attack the ignition switch, the rest of the Pro-start wiring can be assembled. There's a relay, which fits into this socket with black, white, and blue wires

02 off it . . .

This lot needs to be mounted somewhere so it's hidden, but fairly accessible (we've known the fuse to blow, for instance). This is a rather neat solution, using one of the steering column mounting bolts for the relay, and strapping the fuse to

03 . . . and an in-line fuse for the white wire.

04 that.

Before you go any further, now would be a great time to disconnect the battery. The ignition switch wiring is a prime source of volts, and we'll be chopping those wires about some. Better if they're not carrying voltage at

05 the time, really.

Right - no more messing about. Pull the wiring plug off the back of the ignition switch, and we're on

06 our way

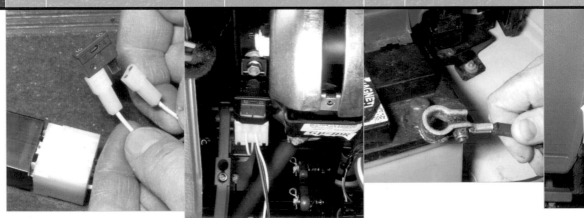

07 On our Punto, we had a big brown wire, which is permanent live. Not interested in that. The big red is the starter feed wire, which we'll come back to. For now, let's concentrate on the big orange wire, which is ignition live. Here we go with our strip-and-solder method - trim off a section of the plastic insulation . . .

08 . . . then bare the end of the white wire, and wrap it round.

09 A little solder, and now there's a solid joint, which is also a lot more reliable than any connector (bit of a bonus, since we're relying on this to start the engine). This is one soldered joint which must be well-insulated, so wrap it with plenty of tape when you're done.

10 Back to the large red wire we found earlier. This one, you can cut an inch or two from the plug . . .

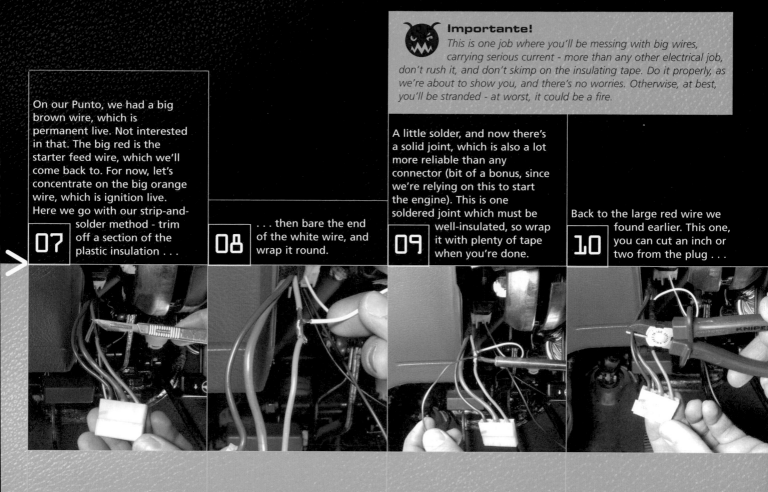

11 . . . and tape the short end up. Leaving it cut like this means the ignition key will no longer start the engine, which is the whole point of a starter button.

12 The other end of our red wire gets joined to the blue wire from the new relay. You could use some large bullet connectors for this, but we like permanent solutions - besides, the soldering iron's hot to trot. Insulate that joint thoroughly - the only place you'll find bigger current is at the battery.

13 Now there's just the button itself to fit and wire up. We're quite proud of our 'carbon-fibre' switch panel (you can probably tell), and the button slips in there like it was made for it. Well, it was - kind-of.

14 Wherever your button's going, make sure there's room behind to fit the retaining nut, and for you to get your hands in, to wire it up.

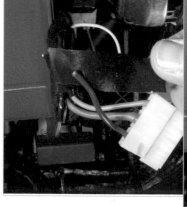

>>

15 The nut doesn't have to be murder-tight, but it's gonna see some action, and we don't want it going floppy on us.

16 Bring the black wire from the relay across the car to your button . . .

17 . . . and connect it up to one side (doesn't matter which).

To complete the starter circuit, we now need a decent earth. Ours is coming from one we made earlier, while fitting our washer jet lights (see 'Body styling'). This is one earth connection where a dodgy self-tapper through the car body might not do the trick - make it good.

18

Run another wire back from your earth point to the other side of the button, and that's it. You are a wiring God.

19

Seeing the starter button nestling in our custom-made switch panel gives us a real warm glow. You'll be nearly as chuffed yourself when your Punto bursts into life. When you're happy it all works, go back and make a neat job of all the wiring - loom it with tape, fix it in place with cable-ties, that sort of thing. Boring, but important.

20

Pedalling your Punto

A tasty race-equipment touch to your modded machine, pedal extensions really look the part when combined with full chequerplate mats, or alloy footwells - available in several styles and (anodised) colours.

Not sure how well the anodising will wear, though… The only other issue with pedals is the clutch and brake must have rubbers fitted - this is first of all sensible (so your feet don't slip off them at an awkward moment) and it's also a legal requirement. Don't buy extensions without.

01 First job is to remove the rubber covers from each pedal. No worries so far.

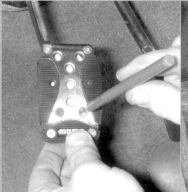

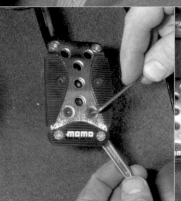

02 Stick some masking tape over the pedal, offer the new extension in place, and mark where to drill the holes. Make sure the holes you have marked are at least 2 mm away from the outside edge of the pedal. Also check that you won't be trying to drill through the pedal arm - you won't get very far, and it's dangerous. Fit at least two bolts per pedal - one won't do.

03 Next job (you guessed it) is to drill the holes. Some newspaper or rags underneath will catch any swarf and make it easier to clean up after. A block of wood behind the pedal stops it moving, and eliminates the chance of you drilling through the carpet. To stop the drill slipping when you start, use a hammer and punch to mark the hole.

04 Next the Allen-headed bolt can be slipped through, with the retaining nut on behind, and the pair tightened. Make sure they're done up tight - loose pedals could mean problems. It's worth checking they're still tight after a few week's caning, too - especially the over-worked throttle pedal.

05 As is the case with most aftermarket pedal kits, the instructions with our Momo Grand Prix pedals state that they must be at least 50 mm apart. It really is important that the pedals are evenly spaced – we're sure everyone can appreciate the complications of having the brake pedal too near the throttle pedal.

Boring flooring?

Alright, so carpets have always been a dull colour because they have to not show the dirt - when was the last time you heard of a car with white carpets? What goes on the floor needn't be entirely dull, though, and can still be easy to clean, if you're worried.

Ripping out the old carpets is actually quite a major undertaking - first, the seats have to come out (you might be fitting new ones anyway), but the carpets and underfelt fit right up under the dashboard, and under all the sill trims and centre console, etc. Carpet acts as sound-deadening, and is a useful thing to hide wiring under, too, so don't be in too great a hurry to ditch it completely. Unless, of course, your Punto is having a full-on race/rally style treatment, in which case - dump that rug!

Chequerplate is the current fashion in cool flooring, and it's easy to see why it'll probably have an enduring appeal - it's tough but flexible, fairly easy to cut and shape to fit, has a cool mirror finish, and it matches perfectly with the racing theme so often seen in the modified world, and with the ally trim that's widely used too.

Tips 'n' tricks
If you're completely replacing the carpet and felt with, say, chequerplate throughout, do this at a late stage, after the ICE install and any other electrical work's been done - that way, all the wiring can be neatly hidden underneath it.

Chequer mats

 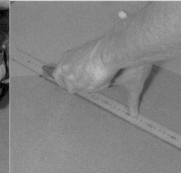 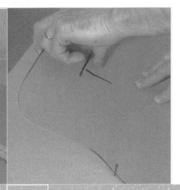

01 The halfway-house to a fully-plated interior is to make up your own tailored mats (you can buy ready-mades if you're not allowed to play with sharp knives). Unless you buy real ally chequer, what you'll get is actually plastic, and must be supported by mounting it on hardboard. Take one of the lovely 'Granny' mats your car might have come with, and use it as a template to mark the shape onto the hardboard (you could always make a template from some thin card).

02 With the shape marked out, it's time for the jigsaw - next to a cordless drill, this has to be one of the most useful tools ever invented for the modder.

03 To make the hardboard fit better into the footwells, score it at the bend where it goes up under the pedals . . .

04 . . . then carefully 'fold' the hardboard back to the required shape - trust us, this will make your new chequer mats fit superbly.

05 Not unlike this in fact. Try your hardboard mat in place, and trim the corners and edges as necessary to get it fitting as flat as poss.

06 Now you can use your hardboard as a template, for cutting out the chequer. Try to make the chequer fractionally bigger overall than the hardboard, so you don't see the wood edge (you shouldn't anyway, if your board is a tidy fit). Stick the chequer to the board, using some decent glue - spray glue's convenient, but usually not quite up to the job. You can't beat good old brush-on Evo-Stik (and no, we're not being paid to say that).

07 Do it right, and you too can have a floor like this - looks sweet, and the mats don't slip. Sorted.

Wheely cool

A new steering wheel is an essential purchase in personalising your Punto. It's one of the main points of contact between you and the car, it's sat right in front of you, and the standard ones are dull and massive!

Don't be tempted to fit too small a wheel - the smaller Puntos never had power steering, and a tiny-rimmed steering wheel will make manoeuvring very difficult, especially with phat tyres.

One bit of good news is that, once you've shelled out for your wheel, it may be possible to fit it to your next car, too. When you buy a new wheel, you usually have to buy a boss (or mount) to go with it - the mounts are less pricey, so one wheel could be fitted to another completely different car, for minimum cost.

A trick feature worth investigating is the detachable wheel/boss. This feature comes in handy when you park up and would rather the car was still there when you come back (something most people find a bonus). It's all very well having a steering wheel immobiliser or steering lock, but I doubt many thieves will be driving off in your car if the steering wheel's completely missing! Also, removing the wheel may remove the temptation to break in and pinch… your wheel!

A word about **airbags**

Which Puntos have airbags? It's a bit of a random feature - from our information, if your Punto's older than February 1995, you probably don't have one. After that, the range-topping models had one as standard, and it was an option for lesser Puntos. So far, the market for replacement wheels with airbags hasn't materialised, so fitting your tasty new wheel means losing what some (old) people think is a valuable safety feature.

So just disconnect the damn thing, right? Wrong. Then your airbag warning light will be on permanently - not only is this irritating, your newly-modded motor will fail the MOT (having the airbag itself isn't compulsory, but if the warning light's on, it's a fail - at least at the time this was written). Two ways round this - either take out the clocks (see the section on fitting white dials) and remove the offending warning light bulb, OR bridge the airbag connector plug pins with two lengths of wire soldered to either side of a 5A fuse. Bridging the pins this way 'fools' the test circuit (which fires up every time you switch on the ignition) into thinking the airbag's still there, and the warning light will go out as it should.

Disabling the airbag is yet another issue which will interest your insurance company, so don't do it without consulting them first. We're just telling you, that's all.

Warning: Airbags are expensive to replace (several £100s), and are classed as an explosive!!! Funny, that - for a safety item, there's any number of ways they can CAUSE injuries or damage if you're not careful - check this lot out:

a Before removing the airbag, the battery MUST be disconnected (don't whinge about it wiping out your stereo pre-sets). When the battery's off, don't start taking out the airbag for another 10 minutes or so. The airbag system stores an electrical charge - if you whip it out too quick, you might set it off, even with the battery disconnected. True.

b When the airbag's out, it must be stored the correct way up.

c The airbag is sensitive to impact - dropping it from sufficient height might set it off. Even if dropping it doesn't actually set it off, it probably won't work again, anyway. By the way, once an airbag's gone off, it's scrap. You can't stuff it back inside.

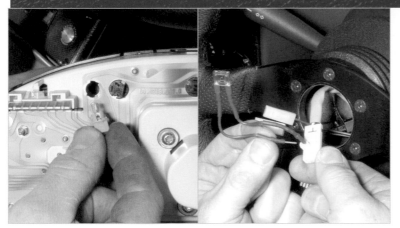

d If you intend to keep the airbag with a view to refitting it at some stage (like when you sell the car), store it in a cool place - but bear in mind that the storage area must be suitable, so that if the airbag went off by accident, it would not cause damage to anything or anyone. Sticking it under your bed might not be such a good idea.

e If you're not keeping the airbag, it must be disposed of correctly (don't just put it out for the bin men!). Contact your local authority for advice.

f Airbags must not be subjected to temperatures in excess of 90°C (194°F) - just remember that bit about airbags being an explosive - you don't store dynamite in a furnace, now do you? Realistically in this country, the only time you'll get THAT hot is in a paint-drying oven.

Removing a non-airbag wheel

If you're lucky enough not to have an airbag, removing the shonky old wheel is much easier - here's how. Start by prising off the horn pad, taking care not to gouge the plastic (if you're intending to refit the old wheel any time). Disconnect the horn wiring plug on the back, then check you've got the front wheels set straight before undoing the steering wheel nut. You'll find that the nut has a collar on top, which has been folded over to pin the nut in place (this is called 'staking' the nut) - use a chisel (or old screwdriver) to tap the folded section of nut back into its original shape, then undo the nut. Don't rely on the steering lock to stop the wheel turning while you unscrew the nut (you'll bust the lock) - use your other hand to hold the wheel rim. Unscrew the nut almost all the way off, then tap the wheel from behind to free it from its splines. When it's free, remove the nut completely, and the old wheel's just a bad memory.

Fitting a
sports wheel

01 Disconnect the battery negative (earth) lead and wait 10 minutes before proceeding to remove the steering wheel. The two airbag Allen bolts are the first things to be removed, from behind the wheel. Turn the steering wheel a quarter-turn either way to gain access to these bolts.

06 Hold the boss in place by fitting a new steering wheel nut. Fiat recommends you use a new one, and this is certainly advisable if your old one looks shot in any way. A drop of Loctite should help keep everything in place nicely for now - we'll fully tighten the nut later (when we've got something to hold on to).

07 To keep the MOT inspector happy and the law off your back, you'll need to make sure the horn works on your new wheel. To make this happen, go back to the old steering wheel and rescue the old horn wiring plug. Cut off the plug and at least two inches of the old earth and live wires.

08 Crimp a female bullet onto the ends of the two wires, then connect the horn plug back into the main wiring plug (sticking up through the boss).

09 The horn adapter plate is the next thing to go into place on the boss . . .

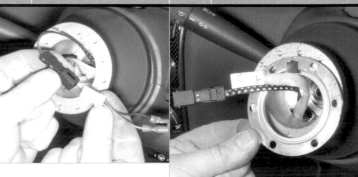

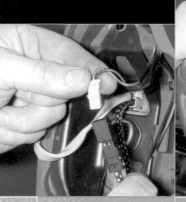

02 Use your fingers to unclip the horn pad, and pull the pad gently towards you. You'll then see the wiring plug for the airbag – this needs to be disconnected. Once this has been done, the airbag can then be removed and stored in a safe place. The kerb next to your car is not a safe place! See 'A word about airbags' for what to do with the wiring.

03 Next job is to disconnect the horn wiring plug - we'll need this again later, so don't lose track of it.

04 Prise off the plastic cap hiding the steering wheel nut. Centralise the wheel, making sure that the front wheels are in the straight-ahead position, then lock the steering (take out the key). Grip the wheel with one hand (don't let the steering lock take the strain) and loosen the nut. Our wheel came off easily enough, but some pulling power may be needed.

05 Feed the horn and airbag wiring through the hole in the boss, and sit the new boss into place on the splines. The boss we're using is non-directional, but many have 'TOP' markings on - check your own fitting instructions.

10 . . . and now the steering wheel can be fitted into place and secured with the Allen bolts. Don't want these left loose, for fairly obvious reasons.

11 With a wheel rim to grab hold of again, find yourself a torque wrench and tighten the steering wheel nut to 50 Nm. If you don't have a torque wrench, do the nut up as tight as you sensibly can. Your life does depend on it, after all.

12 All that's left to do now is pop the horn wire connectors into place on the back of the new horn pad (doesn't matter which way round they go) . . .

13 . . . then press the horn pad into position, taking care not to trap any wires. Now go and see how your new rim feels on the open road - what a difference a wheel makes!

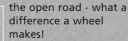

Are you sitting stylishly?

The perfect complement to your lovingly-sorted suspension, because you need something better than the standard seats to hold you in, now that you can corner so much faster... and they look brutal, by way of a bonus. Besides the seat itself, remember to price up the subframe to adapt it to the mounting points in your car. Most people also choose the three- or four-point harnesses to go with it (looks a bit daft to fit a racing seat without it), but make sure the harness you buy is EC-approved, or an eagle-eyed MOT tester might make you take 'em out.

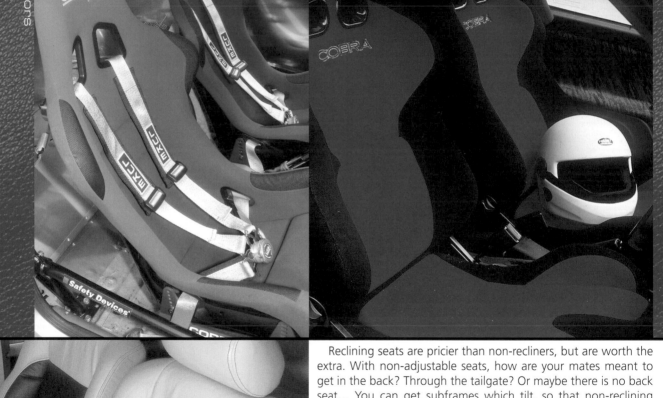

Reclining seats are pricier than non-recliners, but are worth the extra. With non-adjustable seats, how are your mates meant to get in the back? Through the tailgate? Or maybe there is no back seat... You can get subframes which tilt, so that non-reclining seats can move forward. Non-reclining racing seats should be tried for fit before you buy.

An alternative to expensive racing seats would be to have your existing seats re-upholstered in your chosen colours/fabrics, to match your interior theme. You might be surprised what's possible, and the result could be something truly unique. If you've got a basic model, try sourcing seats from a breakers (haggle if the side bolsters are worn away - a common fault). A secondhand interior bought here will be a lot cheaper than buying new goodies, and you know it'll fit easily (all Puntos are the same underneath) - but - it won't have that unique style. Specialist breakers may be able to supply something more rad, such as a leather interior from a top-spec Bravo or Coupé - might take some persuading to get it in, though!

01 Do they stay, or do they go? Quite a big decision in rethinking your Punto's interior, rear seats. Maybe they're making way for a massive ICE install, or perhaps a roll cage? Weight-saving, for max performance? Anyhoo, removal's easy. Fold forward the seat cushion, and remove the Allen bolt on the hinge . . .

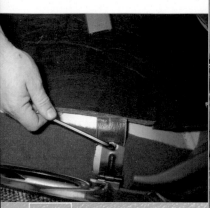

02 . . . and one half of the seat's gone already.

03 On our Punto, the boot carpet was screwed to the base of the seat backrest. With that part of the seat now folded forward, removing the screws was simple.

Rear
seats

04 Another large Allen bolt acts as a pivot on the outside of the backrest - remove it . . .

06 . . . then by tilting the seat, you can unhook each half of the split backrest from the mounts in the centre. Just unbolt the centre mounting from the floor, and you'd never know it was ever there.

Tips 'n' tricks
If you're boarding-out the back of your Punto for an ICE install, use cardboard first to make a template of the required shape, then transfer that to your MDF.

Front seats

Interiors

01 The front seats are secured to the floorpan by four bolts. To remove the two front bolts, use the correct-sized Allen socket and ratchet. Push the chair fully back on its runners to gain better access to the bolts.

02 Next, remove the two rear bolts. To improve access to these bolts, push the chair fully forward on its runners.

03 Surprised he doesn't look happier than that - the nasty standard chair (with 'Sporting' written all over it, in our case) is no more.

07 If you have it, a small amount of Loctite on the seat bolt threads will improve their staying power.

08 Then, in exactly the same way as you removed the seat, fix the new one in place. You can tell these are quality-made seats, because they locate on the existing seat mounting points perfectly. Which is nice.

09 It's common to fit harnesses with bucket seats, but maybe due to a lack of funds (or maybe because you don't like them), you're going without. If so, you need to do a little transplant operation with the seat belt stalk. Start by prising off the rubber cap on the side of the old seat, to reveal the stalk retaining bolt . . .

04 Before we go ahead and fit our new Cobra buckets, the subframes need to be bolted onto the seat. Pop the subframe into place and secure with the four bolts. To get access to the bolts, move the seat runners either fully up or down.

05 Still not looking as happy as he should be - this bucket's a big improvement in almost every way over the old seats.

06 Usually when bolting a new seat into place, you can re-use the original seat bolts. However, we discovered that the Fiat originals were a wee bit on the short side, so you'll need to find yourself some longer bolts, complete with washers.

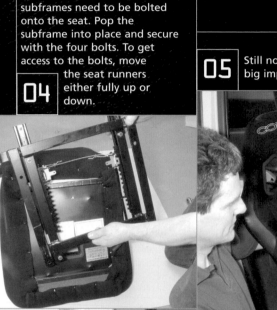

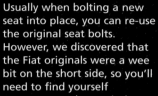

10 . . . then remove this bolt and lift the assembly away from the seat.

11 Into the car now, and locate the stalk assembly on the purpose-made metal bracket on the new subframe. If you don't have anywhere obvious to mount your stalk, ring the seat suppliers and complain - there should be somewhere for it to go. This is one item you can't just 'bodge on'.

12 All that's left is to tighten the bolt up, and you're finished. You now have working seatbelts to tide you over until you decide to fit harnesses. Not that we're trying to pressure you, or anything.

Fitting harnesses

It's true that not everyone likes racing harnesses, but anyone like that's just boring, or should probably eat less pies. Besides, you don't fit sexy race seats and then not fit race belts, do you?

The only problem with harnesses is caused by where you have to mount them. Even with a three-point harness, you end up using one of the rear seat belt mounts, and it seriously reduces your ability to carry bodies in the back seats (webbing everywhere). The MOT crew say that, if you've got rear seats, you must have rear seat belts fitted, so you either 'double-up' on your rear belt mounts (use the same mounting bolts for your harnesses and rear belts), or you take the back seats out altogether. Removing the rear seats leaves the rear deck free for chequerplate, speakers, roll cages - whatever you like. It's just important to understand how fundamental harnesses can end up being, to the whole look of your car - there's almost no half-measures with race belts, so you've got to really want 'em.

One thing you must **not** do is to try making up your own seat belt/harness mounting points. Fiat structural engineers spent plenty of time selecting mounting points and testing them for strength. Drilling your own holes and sticking bolts through is fine for mounting speakers and stuff, but you're heading for an interview with the Grim Reaper if you try it with seat belts. The forces in a big shunt are immense. We're not convinced either that the practice of slinging harnesses round a rear strut brace is kosher, from the safety angle - some of the strut braces available are so flimsy (they're usually ally) you can bend them in your hands. Nuts to trusting my life to one of those!

01 With the rear seats removed (see earlier in this section for info), you'll see the rear seat belt mounting bolts. The new harness shoulder straps use the rear seat belt mounting points directly behind each front seat, so your next job is to remove the seatbelts. Begin by prising off the protective plastic cap, then use a 17mm spanner on the two seat belt bolts . . .

02 . . . you'll see that there are two washers attached, one normal and one shakeproof. Our Cobra harnesses have new bolts supplied in the kit (nice touch), so we're only re-using the old washers. Select the correct shoulder strap, remembering that they must be routed to the mounting point in a straight line. Fit the bolt and washers like this, and do them up tight.

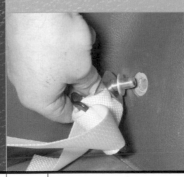

03 Do the same for the strap that will be mounted to the seat belt mount on the rear wheel arch. Make sure the strap's not twisted. Don't be shy about tightening these bolts (they're big enough, and can take it) - there's no torque quoted by Fiat.

04 The harness inner lap straps use the mounting points normally used by the front seat belt stalks. Feed the strap down to the mounting point next to the centre console, then secure the strap in place using the nut and bolt, which will need a spanner each. Do we need to mention they should be tight? Thought not.

05 The outer lap strap is mounted to the front bolt hole from the seat belt sliding rail, at the base of the B-pillar. To remove the rail, prise away the plastic covers and remove the retaining bolts. Note the way the washers are arranged on the bolts, and keep them for the next step.

06 Making sure the strap doesn't get twisted, feed it down to the mounting point, fit the bolt and washers, and tighten up. It's up to you to decide what you're going to do with the original front and rear seat belts. We left them in place, and just poked the ends of the belts down inside the B- and C-pillar trim panels. Why make life difficult?

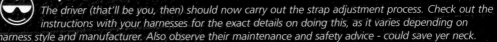

Importante!
The driver (that'll be you, then) should now carry out the strap adjustment process. Check out the instructions with your harnesses for the exact details on doing this, as it varies depending on harness style and manufacturer. Also observe their maintenance and safety advice - could save yer neck.

Fire drill

Fire extinguisher

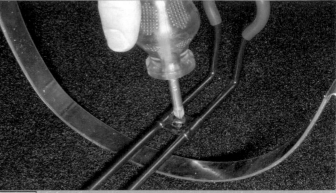

Looking for more inspiration for racing Punto must-haves? It's over to our friends at Safety Devices.

Besides being masters of all things cage-y, this one-stop-shop for competition car safety also know fire extinguisher systems intimately. If you've done the race look, and removed the rear seats, that rear floor area could be looking a bit vacant right now. You might plan to fill it with ICE, but we chose fire.

 01 The first job is to mark and drill two mounting holes for the bracket that holds the fire extinguisher. Before you screw the bracket into place, thread the two straps that hold the bottle in place, under the bracket.

Finally press the quick-release strap catches down to secure the bottle in place and you are done. Should you ever need to use the extinguisher in the future, all you do is flick up the quick-release catches and lift the bottle out. Read the operating instructions on the bottle before you have to use it. Also, don't use it on a fire it's not designed for.

For a proper race-car install (a plumbed-in extinguisher, where the engine bay's protected), Safety Devices can supply all the kit you need. Like flexible tubing (which you run from the bottle into the engine bay), and two nozzles (attach the tubing to these, then mount above fire-risk areas, like the fuel rail).

Lastly, there's a pull-cable to set the thing off, which you mount on the dash.

 02 Lower the fire extinguisher into place.

03

04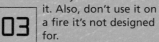

05

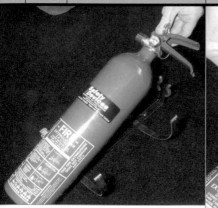

ICE
Headset

The cheaper your Punto, the nastier your standard head unit's going to be. Course, by the time a Punto has passed through several owners, it's pretty unlikely to still have a standard set in anyway, but if all you've got is a hole, don't feel too bad. Standard sets are fine if all you want to do is aimlessly listen to the radio with your arm out the window, but not - definitely not - if you want to impress your mates with the depth and volume of your bass.

In most cases, if you want to listen to CDs, it's got to go - and there's plenty of decent headsets out there which will give you a night-and-day difference in sound quality and features. The headset is the heart of your new install - always go for the best you can afford. Ask the experts which features matter most, if you're building a full system. And don't just go for the look!

Our new Pioneer 5530MP headset is pretty typical of the current single-CD state of the art - decent looks, good sound, plenty of features.

01 First, the old set's got to be shifted. Resist the urge to just crowbar the thing out of the dash - you'll be needing two of the standard radio removal tools to do the job with less damage. And you could always sell it, or keep it, to stick back in when you sell the car? Our stock set won't fit anything except a Punto, as it's got a moulded front panel (meant to discourage theft).

02 Another reason not to get too excited when removing the old set is that most of the wiring behind is fully 'recyclable' - ie we'll be using it again. One bonus on our Punto - it's got ISO plugs for power and speakers, meaning our new set should plug straight in.

03 The old cage has to go too - you can't use this with your new set, or the locking pins won't engage. Most DIY-fitted cages have absolutely every last locking tab bent over, which makes it a long job with a small screwdriver to remove it.

04 With the old cage out of the picture, now's a good time to introduce the new set's cage into the equation . . .

05 . . . and secure it by bending over just a few of the triangular lugs (not all of them!).

06 Having ISO plugs makes life much easier - one does power, the other speakers (the power one has red, yellow and black leads, among others). Here, we're plugging in the original speaker wiring plug to the new headset wiring . . .

07 . . . and now, we're cutting the original speaker wires. Why? We're going to run our rear 6x9s off the headset, so . . .

08 . . . we'll be joining on some decent speaker wire to run to the back of the car. By using the new headset's wiring instructions (these tell you which colour wires are front/rear, positive/negative), when you connect the original speaker plug, you can work out which of the original speaker wires did what. For more wiring info, see 'Wiring up' later in this section.

ICE wiring colour codes

Black plug (power/earth)
Red - 12V permanent live
Yellow - radio memory live
Black - earth
Blue - Remote/P-cont
Orange - dimmer

Brown plug (speakers)
White pair - front left
Grey pair - front right
Green pair - rear left
Purple pair - rear right

>>

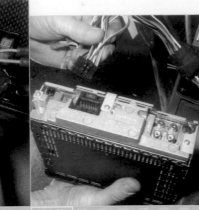

09 Any original speaker wires you're not using should be chopped and taped-up. If you're running all your new speakers amped, just leave the original ISO speaker plug disconnected.

10 Feeling confident now, so we're bringing in the new headset for the first time - plugging in the new wiring is one of the simpler jobs. It's a bit vital to the plot, this plug, so make sure it clips in tight.

11 Power to the headset comes straight from the old ISO wiring plug (this provides permanent and ignition lives, and an earth). Plug this into your headset wiring socket, and it's hot (so leave the ignition key off for now).

12 Virtually all headsets provide an output for remotely switching-on your amps (or for powering-up an electric aerial). Called the 'remote' or 'P-cont' wire, it's usually blue, and should be joined to your own wire which will run back to the amps. One of our RCA leads has a built-in P-cont, so we'd be pretty stupid not to use it.

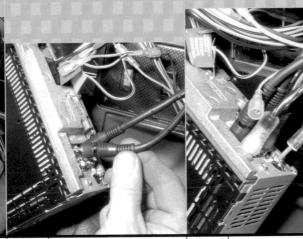

13 When you're confronted with a mass of wiring you can't sort out, don't forget the manual (the Pioneer one, in our case). Our man's got the right idea. Well, it's a lot better than blowing up your headset.

14 Those amps of yours need a signal to work from, and that's what the RCA outputs on the headset provide. If your set's got more than one pair of connections (pre-outs), these may be marked 'front', 'rear' or 'sub'. Use whichever set makes sense for your system. Connect the plug with the red stripe to the red socket - we think you can guess where the other one goes.

15 Don't forget to plug in the aerial lead if you plan on listening to Hip-Hop FM. Grrrreat. If the lead won't fit, you might need an adapter plug. Or you might find (like us) that an adapter plug's been fitted to your lead - all you need do then is take it off.

16 Test that everything's working at this point, before pushing the unit right into its cage. If all's well, push the headset home until it clicks. If it gets stuck, take the set out, and un-bunch all the wiring by hand. Do not force it in, or you could end up having a very bad day. If you have trouble, unclipping the carpet from the front of the centre console gets you in behind. Success? Now get out the instruction manual again, and set those levels properly. Enjoy.

Front speakers

The standard items in the Punto speak volumes (hur-hur) about any car manufacturer's desire to build things down to a price - ie spend as little as poss. What does it cost Fiat for the speakers in a Punto? If it's more than a fiver a set, they're being robbed. Low on power, and with nasty paper cones which disintegrate after a few years, fitting any aftermarket speakers is going to be an upgrade.

So what are your options? Well, unless you've got plans for mahoosive door builds to take some 6x9s or the odd sub, you're limited to co-axial speakers (tweeter and woofer combined) or components (separate woofer and tweeter, with a crossover box). Components usually give the best sound, but you'll need space in your door for a tweeter, and the crossover also needs a home. Tricky. We're taking the easy option, with some quality Pioneer co-axials.

Tricks 'n' tips
When you're shopping for door speakers, check the quoted mounting depth for your chosen components. Based on our experience, the maximum depth you'll get in the Punto front doors, without spacers, is 60 mm.

01 Sorting the speakers on a Punto is so easy. You don't even have to remove the door trim panel first (maybe they're so ashamed of the standard speakers, they decided not to make 'em hard to rip out). Prise off the plastic grille . . .

02 . . . then remove four screws . . .

>>

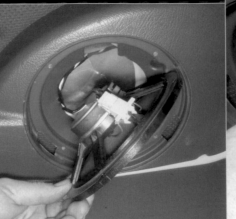

03 . . . and pull off the wiring plug. Those tattered paper cones should burn quite well…

04 Houston, we have a problem. We wanted some front speakers which could kick some butt, but unfortunately, the huge magnets on the back of our 220W Pioneers are just too deep for our doors. They're also too phat, meaning some loss of metalwork in the door area is required before they'll slot in.

05 The lack of depth in our Punto door means we'll need a spacer. You can buy these ready-made from ICE dealers, but we were sort-of in a hurry, so we made our own from MDF. Mark round the outside of the speaker . . .

Now the MDF spacer's finished, so let's try it in the door. A little trimming of the speaker hole at the back, and it's ready for final installation. **09**

We used these DIY-store clamps to hold the MDF spacer up to the back of the speaker, to drill through the four mounting holes. **10**

On with the speaker wiring. The large terminal's positive, and will eventually be joined to our oxygen-free wire with the writing or stripe on it. **11**

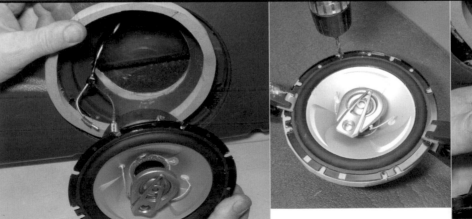

Importante!
MDF dust is nasty stuff to breathe in. Wear a mask when you're cutting, drilling or sanding it.

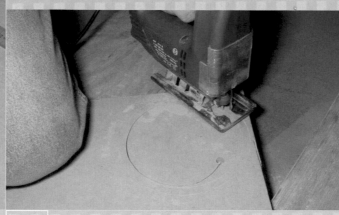

06 . . . use compasses (or dividers) to mark the inner circle - 10 mm inside on our Pioneers . . .

07 . . . then take your steadiest hand to the jigsawing arena, and cut out your spacer. This MDF's the 10 mm thick variety - other thicknesses are available. Remember - always check speaker depths with the front window rolled all the way down, as it's speaker magnet-to-glass clearance we're interested in.

08 Meanwhile, back at the door, no-one's noticed we've cheated with the speaker wiring. Okay, for the ultimate in SPL, you should run oxygen-free (or better) right through into the door, to your speaker. In practice, even pro installers sometimes don't bother. Use your Haynes manual wiring diagram to identify the pos and neg Fiat wires, and crimp on suitable terminals.

If you don't run the oxygen-free wires right into the doors, they have to be joined to the Fiat originals at some point. Either trace the door wiring just inside the car (the footwell area), or do like us, and chop off the Fiat wiring at the ISO plug just behind the headset. **12** Why make life complicated?

For even better sound, the real enthusiasts among you will strip off your door cards (see 'Interiors') and Dynamat all the door metalwork, to kill vibration, before finally fitting the speakers. You'll possibly need longer screws than the ones provided (especially if your spacer's even thicker than 10 mm), but **13** what's four long-ish self-tappers to a DIY master like you, eh?

Now that's a sweet result. We've got a 220W door speaker in there, with no cheating (apart from some skinny Fiat wiring), and it really looks the nuts. Let's **14** feed it some tunes, and see how it sounds.

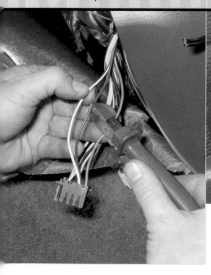

Rear speakers

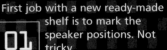

01 First job with a new ready-made shelf is to mark the speaker positions. Not tricky.

If we're talking about a set of 6x9s, rear shelf-mounting is the simplest option. If you don't want to butcher your standard shelf (always a flimsy item), either make a new one from MDF (using your stock shelf as a template), or buy a ready-made acoustic 'stealth' shelf. Either way, make hiding your new speakers a priority - tasty speakers on display in the back window could soon mean no rear window, and no speakers...

While shelf mounting has its advantages, Puntos have another top spot for speakers - the rear side trim panels. Okay for speakers without huge, heavy magnets, you just cut a suitable-sized hole in the panel, and mount your speaker in from behind.

As we're ditching the rear seats on our Punto, we've made up an MDF rear seat panel in place of the old seat backrest - firmly fixed in place, this makes an ideal home for some 6x9s. Maybe even two sets?

Remember that the length of wire to each speaker should be the same (as near as poss), or you might find the speakers run slightly out of phase. Crimp on the right terminals, and connect up your speakers. For max neatness, use P-clips screwed along the edge of the shelf. To remove the shelf more easily, fit some bullet connectors in the speaker wiring, or ask your ICE dealer for a Neutrik connector plug.

02 With a speaker outline marked, remove the wood from the rest of the shelf, and drill a nice big hole somewhere inside the outline... then get busy with the jigsaw.

03 Use the speaker mounts (or even the speakers themselves) as a template to drill the mounting holes . . .

04 . . . then screw on the speakers themselves. Don't forget that 6x9s can be run off the headset, to provide a little 'rear fill' - if you have them amped-up, you might find that the sound's too biased to the back of the car.

05

Importante!
MDF dust is nasty stuff to breathe in. Wear a mask when you're cutting, drilling or sanding it.

Importante!
MDF dust is nasty stuff to breathe in. Wear a mask when you're cutting, drilling or sanding it.

MDF back panel 6x9s

01 For those of you who've never noticed before (possibly because it's on the bit you throw away), speaker manufacturers usually provide a handy cardboard template for fitting their products. It's on the back of the box they come in. Just cut it out . . .

02 . . . and stick it onto your chosen piece of MDF. Drill a hole large enough to take your jigsaw blade, and you're all set. One speaker-sized hole, coming up.

03 Proper templates (like this Kenwood example) also give you guidance for drilling the speaker mounting holes.

04 So - the holes have been cut/drilled, and the panel's been neatly trimmed using spray glue and black carpet. Does the speaker fit? You betcha.

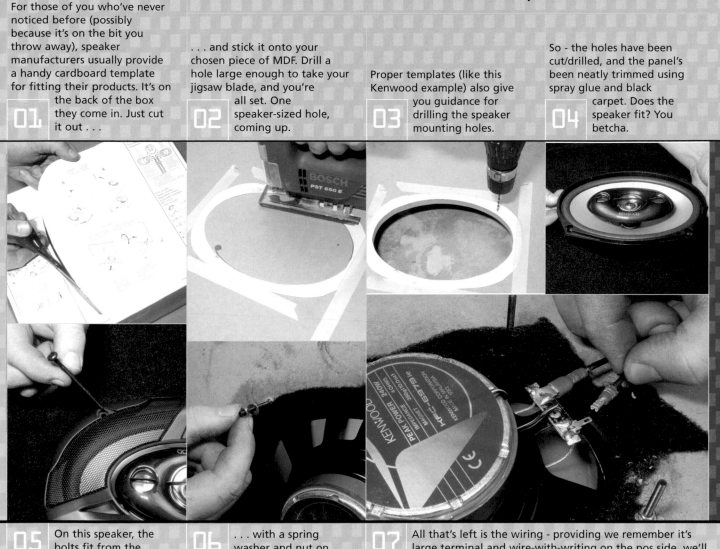

05 On this speaker, the bolts fit from the front . . .

06 . . . with a spring washer and nut on behind.

07 All that's left is the wiring - providing we remember it's large terminal and wire-with-writing on the pos side, we'll soon be hearing sweet, sweet music.

Subs & boxes

No system's complete without that essential deep bass boom and rumble. Don't muck about with bass tubes - get the real thing to avoid disappointment. So you lose some of your boot space - so what? Is getting the shopping in an issue? We think not.

Most people opt for the easy life when it comes to boxes, at least until they're ready for a full-on mental install. The Punto at least has a roomy boot, so standard boxes will fit easily. Making up your own box isn't hard though, especially if you were any good at maths and geometry. Oh, and woodwork. Most subs come with instructions telling you what volume of box they work best in, but ask an expert (or a mate) what they think - the standard boxes are just fine, and none are pricey. The only real reason to build your own is if you've got an odd-shaped boot (or want something that looks trick).

Importante!
MDF dust is nasty stuff to breathe in. Wear a mask when you're cutting, drilling or sanding it.

Tricks 'n' tips
You don't want a heavy sub box sliding about in your boot, so nail it down somehow. Velcro might stop it sliding on the boot carpet, but it's still a bit inadequate - how firmly is the boot carpet attached? In a bad accident, that heavy sub box could go flying - if it connected with your bonce, it'd be lights out. Try using some of those little metal corner brackets you can get from the DIY store, and really pin that box down. Might even improve the sound!

01 Take one standard sub box, and try the sub for size. Don't go fitting it yet, just make sure the hole's big enough for your needs. If not, have they sent you the wrong box? Minor trimmage can be accomplished using a file, or if it's a bit more than minor, use a jigsaw.

02 Once we're sure the sub's a good fit, it can come out again. Forgetting to wire up your sub before fitting it is a very common mistake, caused by being too keen. Most ready-made boxes come fitted with a terminal plate on the side of the box - with these, just run your speaker wire from the sub to the inside of the plate (keep the pos and neg wiring the right way round).

The terminal plates have either screw-type or spring-type terminals for connecting your speaker wire. You can just strip the end, twist it up and shove it in. Or you can 'tin' the end of your speaker wire, with solder, which makes it easier to fit your speaker wire, and removes the chance of any stray strands (which could touch, and blow a channel on your amp or headset). Keeping to our wiring convention, we're joining the writing-on wire to the positive (red) terminal.

Make sure the sub's logo is lined up correctly (this won't affect the sound, just the pose-value), then drill through the mounting holes round the edge of the sub.

03

04 Once the mounting holes are made, screw the sub down tight (unless you want bass all over the place).

05

Wiring-up

For most people, this is the scariest part of an install - just the thought of masses of multi-coloured spaghetti sticking out of your dash might have you running to the experts (or a knowledgeable mate). But - if you do everything in a logical order, and observe a few simple rules, wiring-up isn't half as brain-numbing as it seems.

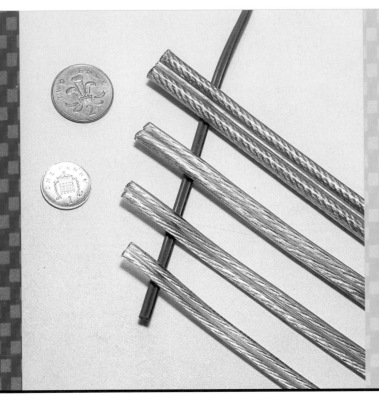

Live feeds

Although a typical head unit can be powered off the standard Fiat wiring (the stock wire is good for about 15 amps, tops) running amplifiers means you'll be needing a new live feed, taken straight off the battery. Or in our case, straight off the junction box we fitted as part of our fusebox install (see 'security').

Get some decent 'eight-gauge' (quite heavy) or 'four-gauge' (getting on for battery cable thickness - serious stuff) wire, and a matching fuseholder. If you're running more than one item off this feed wire, get a distribution block too, which splits the feed up, with a separate fuse for each item - who'd have thought electrical safety can look trick too?

Pub trivia

Hands up, who knows what 'RCA' stands for? We use it every day in ICE-speak, but WHAT does it really mean? Really Clever Amplifier lead? Remote Control Acoustic lead? Well, the answer's a strange one. RCA leads and connectors are also known as 'phono' connectors in the world of TV and hi-fi, and they've been around a long, long time. How long, exactly? We're talking back in the days when you could only get radios - big suckers with valves in them, and long before anyone thought of putting one in a car. RCA actually stands for Radio Corporation of America, who hold the patent on this type of connector and lead. Not a lot of people know that.

Speaker and RCA wiring

As with all wiring, the lesson here is to be neat and orderly - or - you'll be sorry! RCA leads and speaker wires are prone to picking up interference (from just about anywhere), so the first trick to learn when running ICE wiring is to keep it away from live feeds, and also if possible, away from the car's ECUs (the main one's right out of the way, under the bonnet). Another way to interference-hell is to loop up your wiring, when you find you've got too much (we've all been there). Finding a way to lose any excess lengths of wire without bunching can be an art - laying it out in a zig-zag, taping it to the floor as you go, is just one solution.

Another lesson in neatness is finding out what kinds of cable clips are available, and where to use them. There's various stick-on clips which can be used as an alternative to gaffer tape on floors, and then 'P-clips', which look exactly as their name suggests, and can be screwed down (to speaker shelves, for instance). 'Looming'

your wiring is another lesson well-learned - this just means wrapping short strips of tape around, particularly on pairs of speaker wires or RCAs. As we've already said, don't loom speaker wire with power cables (or even with earths).

The last point is also about tidiness - mental tidiness. When you're dealing with speaker wiring, keep two ideas in mind - positive and negative. Each speaker has a pos (+) and neg (-) terminal. Mixing these up is not an option, so work out a system of your own, for keeping positive and negative in the right places on your headset and amp connections. Decent speaker cable is always two wires joined together - look closely, and you'll see that one wire has writing (or a stripe) on, and the other is plain. Use the wire with writing for pos connections throughout your system, and you'll never be confused again. While we're at it, RCA leads have red and white connector plugs - Red is for Right.

01 If you're running a live feed straight from the battery, you'll need to get it into the car at some point. Have a look at the fusebox fitting section in 'security' to see how we did ours. You'll also need an in-line fuseholder . . .

02 . . . containing a fuse that'll cover the total load for your system.

03 There's something really satisfying about this type of fuseholder - it's just made for the job. Pop the bared end of your eight-gauge wire in the other end, and clamp it with the Allen-headed grub screw. Now that's quality. Remember, though - as soon as the fuseholder's connected up, the other end of that wire is live (even if the ignition's off).

04 Removing the centre console's a top idea to make running the ICE wiring down the car easier. Unclip a couple of plastic panels front and rear, and you'll find a total of three nuts - undo these, and the console can be lifted up enough to work in there.

05 After a little "minor" surgery to the front part of the console . . .

06 . . . the RCAs can be fed in through our new holes, and on past the handbrake to the back of the car. We've removed our back seat (see 'Interiors'), which makes things easier still, but it's not essential.

07 Alternatively, route the wires down the sides of the car. After unclipping the sill trim/door seal, you'll be surprised how much wire can be hidden this way. Keep the power feeds and speaker wires separate by running them down the other side. If your sill trims are secured using screws, be careful when refitting - a screw through the wiring is a good way to kill your system.

Amplifiers

01 First, we need power - masses of power. Here, we're splitting the main power feed from the front of the car into two, using this rather neat circuit-breaker instead of the more usual distribution block.

02 The all-important live supply is one amp connection you should really use a proper terminal on, rather than just stuffing a bare wire into the hole. And insulate any bare metal on the terminal - that live touches anything else, and the results won't be good.

So, how many amps do we want in our car? One school of thought says each pair of speakers, and each sub, should have an individual amp - by setting the output from each amp separately, you can control each aspect of the sound, before you even need to think about adding a graphic equaliser. You can also better match your speakers to the level of power they need, to work best. Trouble is, running several amps means doubling-up on wiring, and you could end up drawing a monster amount of power from that battery.

Any starter system can be made to seriously kick, using just one 400W four-channel amp - choose the right one carefully (and the components to go with it), and just one will do. With a 'tri-mode' amp, you could run your front components off one pair of channels, bridge the other two for a sub, and run some rear 6x9s off the head unit. Don't forget that decent modern headsets chuck out fifty-per-channel now, so don't assume you'll need separate amps for everything. Ideally, in any system, the sound shouldn't all come from behind you - ears were designed to work best with sound arriving from in front (and who are we to argue?).

Decide where you'll mount the amps carefully. Any amp must be adequately cooled - don't cover it up so there's no airflow, and don't hang it upside-down from your shelf.

Our system set-up uses two matching Sony Xplod amps - one 1000W beast for our sub, and a 480W two-channel for the front speakers. They've got the look, but how about the performance to back it up? Let's find out.

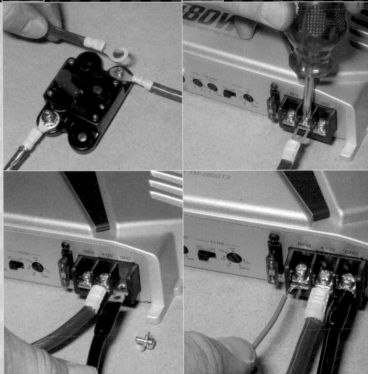

06 Don't use skinny wires for earths - ideally, it should be the same-thickness wire as you've used for your live feed. Connecting it to the amp's the easy bit (make sure it's done up tight).

07 Next up, it's the humble P-cont (remote) lead going on. This performs the vital function of carrying the 'switch-on' signal from your headset - without this, you won't hear much. The good news is, this is one time when size doesn't matter - it doesn't carry much current, so the wire can be as skinny as you like.

Before we can connect up the earth, we need a decent earth point somewhere in the boot, to join our wire to. A quick spot of drillage in the rear of the Punto boot . . .

03

. . . followed by slipping in a nut and bolt, securely tightened . . .

04

. . . and now we've got an earth point we can add any number of wires to, secured with a second nut. No dodgy self-tappers here, then.

05

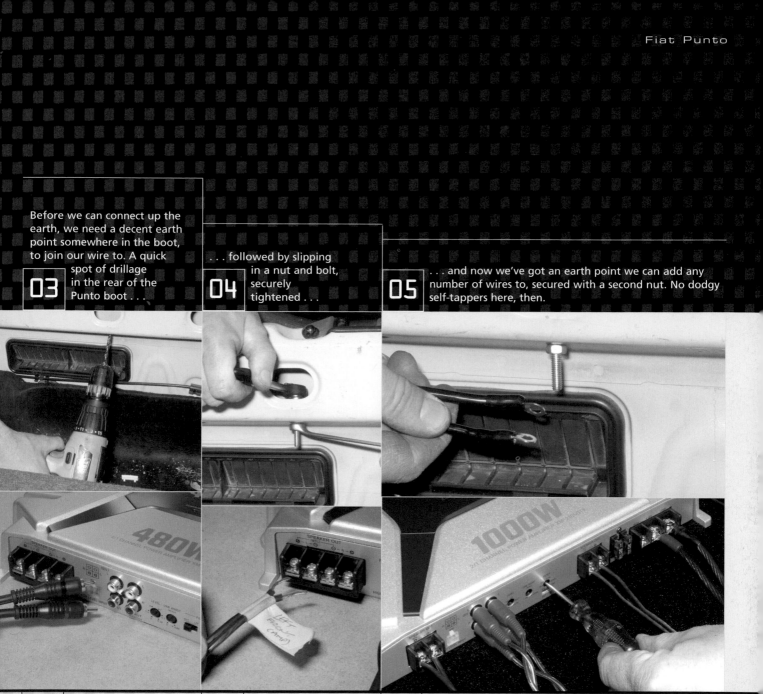

08 Connecting up the RCAs shouldn't tax your brain too much. This amp has a pass-through facility, meaning you could run another RCA lead out of this amp, into another one. We just want the input connections for this install. Not all RCA leads are marked red and white, but there will be one colour on one lead, to avoid embarrassing mistakes.

09 Read the amp's instruction book carefully when connecting any wires, or you might regret it, especially for bridged or tri-mode. Identify your speaker pos and neg/left and right wires with a piece of tape, and get them screwed on. As with the lives and earths, it's also vital there's no stray bits of wire left poking out.

10 A good tip is to leave the amps loose until after you've set them up - if you can, leave good access to the gain adjustment (volume) screws after final fitting, too. Starting at normal listening volume, with the amp gain turned down, put on a kicking track, then turn the gain up until the speakers just start to distort. Turn the gain down a tad from there, and you've a good basic setting. Amp gain and headset faders can now be tweaked to give a good balanced sound - or whatever tickles your lugholes.

Tricks 'n' tips
Very few systems work 100%, first time. If the amp LEDs don't light up, for instance, are they getting power? Are the P-cont/remote wires connected properly? If the sub doesn't kick, is the amp switch set to bridged or tri-mode, not stereo? Are the low-pass switches in the correct position? RTFM.

Engines

Faster, faster!

So - does your car talk the talk (sounds fast), or does it walk the walk (actually is fast)? There's no shame in just having a fast-sounding car - not everyone can afford mega-performance, which is why bolt-on goodies like induction kits and big-bore exhausts are such big business. Serious engine tuning costs, and not just in the engine parts - your insurance company will throw a wobbly at a gas-flowed head, and might refuse to cover you altogether if you go for that 200 bhp GT engine conversion.

The induction kit and sports exhaust are an essential first choice, and usually it's as far as you can really go before your insurance company disowns you. Both mods help the engine to 'breathe' better, which helps when you go for the accelerator initially, improving the response you feel, while you also get a crowd-pleasing induction roar and rasp from the back box, so everyone's happy.

Now for the harsh and painful truth. On their own, an induction kit and back box may not gain you much extra 'real' power. Sorry, but it's a myth. Time and again, people fit induction kits and back boxes, expecting huge power gains, and those 'in the know' have a quiet chuckle. All these things really do is make the car sound sportier, and improve the response - accept this, and you won't be disappointed. Ask yourself why most insurance companies don't generally increase premiums for the likes of a performance rear box or induction kit. The answer is - because (on their own) they don't make enough difference!

The 'bolt-on' performance goodies have more effect as part of an engine 'makeover' package, and setting-up the engine properly after fitting these parts can make a huge difference. If you're halfway serious about increasing the go of your Punto, talk to someone with access to a rolling road, so you can prove what's been done has actually made a useful gain. If you've spent time and a ton of money on your car, of course you're going to think it feels faster, but is it actually making more power?

Fitting all the performance goodies in the world will be pretty pointless if the engine's already knackered, but it might not be as bad as you think. One of the best ways to start on the performance road is simply to ensure that the car's serviced properly - new spark plugs, filters, and an oil change, are a good basis to begin from. Correct any obvious faults, such as hoses or wiring plugs hanging off, and look for any obviously-damaged or leaking components, too.

Breathe with me...

Replacement **element**

One of the simplest items to fit, the replacement air filter element has been around for years - of course, now the induction kit's the thing to have, but a replacement element is more discreet (if you're worried about such things).

While we're at it, don't listen to anyone who says just take out the air filter completely - this is a really naff idea. The fuel system's air intake acts like a mini vacuum cleaner, sucking in air from the front of the car, and it doesn't just suck in air, but also dust, dirt and leaves. Without a filter, all this muck would end up in the sensitive parts of the fuel system, and will quickly make the car undriveable. Worse, if any of it makes it into the engine, this will lead to engine wear. Remember too, that cheaper performance filters can be of very suspect quality - if your new filter disintegrates completely inside six months, it'll do wonders for the airflow, but it'll also be letting in all sorts of rubbish!

Some performance filters have to be oiled before fitting - follow the instructions provided; don't ignore this part, or the filter won't be effective. If the filter won't fit, check whether you actually have the right one - don't force it in, and don't cut it to fit, as either of these will result in gaps, which would allow unfiltered air to get in.

Induction kit

You'd either have to be mad, or without a pulse, not to want more performance from your car, and freeing up your engine's breathing is one way to start. Pipercross have been one of the top names in induction and air filtration for many years, because they have a great reputation for producing quality goods. What the increased cool air flow from a complete induction kit will do is tell the engine ECU that it needs to add more fuel, which it will do (in small amounts). This will result in a quick-revving, throaty-sounding engine, with (maybe) more power and more torque. So, you're waiting for what exactly?

01 First job is to remove the three bolts that secure the front of the air filter housing to the body of the car.

02 Loosen the hose clip, and separate the inlet duct from the air box.

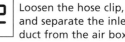

Tricks 'n' tips
On GT models (which suffer from higher underbonnet temperatures than lesser Puntos), feeding the induction kit cone with cold air is even more important. Getting cold air into the engine will also make life easier for the intercooler, and should give you the power boost you're looking for.

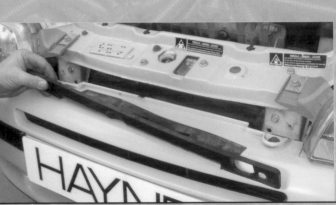

03 Unclip the air inlet hose from its mounting point in the inner wing. The inlet hose and air box are now free to be lifted away from the car - and out of sight!

04 For an extra tweak, remove the two retaining bolts that secure a plastic cover in between the two headlights. Once removed, more cold air will be let into the system, which all helps improve the performance of your car's engine.

Installing the power cone is really easy and takes very little time. Fix the large support bracket supplied in the kit to the first pillar of the existing air box mounting point.

05

Next, the special hose clip with its integral mounting bracket slips over the end of the inlet duct . . .

06

. . . then the stud on the hose clip is located into the large support bracket, and is held in place with a Nyloc nut.

07

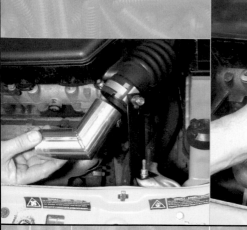

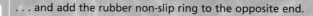

08 Slide the stainless steel adapter pipe into the inlet hose . . .

09 . . . and add the rubber non-slip ring to the opposite end.

10 Before you go any further, you may have noticed that you have a spray can of filter oil supplied with this kit - give the cone a good spray of oil now. Pipercross are unusual in having this - most induction kits we've used come pre-oiled. Still, it's kinda fun this way (if a bit messy).

11 Slide the filter and a hose clip into place on the adapter pipe, and tighten the hose clip securely. Now tighten the other hose clip, and the nuts on the support brackets (if you haven't already).

12 You may have spotted a length of flexi pipe in the kit - guessed what it's for yet? Of course - it's the cold-air feed pipe. Without this, you're losing half the point of an induction kit. Fitting points in the Punto's engine bay are limited, but don't let that deter you. First, there's a trumpet-style end piece to fit to each end of the tube, secured in place with a hose clip.

13 We fitted our new cold-air feed into the inner wing, where the old air inlet hose was. Cable-ties will help hold the tube in place. Now bark up the engine, and blip that throttle. Impressed?

Finally...
Once you've fitted your new filter or induction kit, even if you don't take the car to a rolling road for setting up, at least take it to a garage and have the emissions checked - any minor adjustments should ensure that the engine will, if nothing else, still tick over okay, and should ensure an MOT emissions pass.

01 Why not remove the resonator box located on top of the engine? This is a great idea, introducing the possibility of painting the rocker cover, or fitting coloured HT leads - it just makes the engine bay look better. Remove the two bolts and washers, and the box is free to be lifted away.

02 The two holes left from the resonator box can be plugged by refitting the bolts you just removed.

A little less induction 'kit'

You'll need to find a way of plugging the hole in the air duct where the resonator box branched off. Why not slide a spray can black plastic top the right size into the hole . . . **03**

04 . . . and cable-tie it in place? All it's got to be is fairly air-tight.

05 Last job is to unbolt the large metal support bracket located at the front of the rocker cover, and you're done. There - doesn't that look better?

Other air filter-type mods

One old favourite, if you haven't gone for an induction kit, is drilling holes in the air filter box. Only drill the air filter box below the level where the filter element sits, or the air going into the engine won't be filtered. Making your airbox look like a Swiss cheese won't make the car faster, but it does give you the nice throaty induction roar at full throttle.

HT leads

Engine dress items are always important for creating that individual look, plus most items even claim to improve power output. Don't think we're going to get much increase in performance out of these Mega Leads, but they do look the part. First job in fitting these - remove the air cleaner or resonator (see 'induction kit').

01 To prevent the possibility of mixing the spark plug leads, change one at a time. Begin by lifting out the HT lead.

02 Trace the wire down towards the coil, unclipping it from the clips on the cylinder head cover. Yes, this looks suspiciously like a Ford, but the idea's the same on a Fiat.

03 Disconnect the lead from the ignition coil by pulling it off the end of the coil terminal. With the original HT lead in one hand, go through the new kit to find the lead that matches the original in length, and refit the new lead in the same way as you removed the old one. And that's it, simply repeat this process for the remaining three leads.

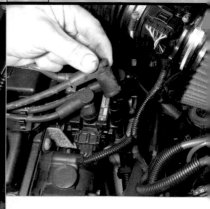

Adjustable fuel pressure regulator
(power boost valve)

These valves allow the fuel system pressure to be increased over the standard regulator valve. Contrary to what you might think, they don't actually provide much more fuel (this is regulated separately by the injection ECU). The effect of increasing the injection pressure is to improve the injector spray pattern, which helps the fuel to burn more efficiently, and has the effect of increasing engine power while actually reducing emission levels.

To see the true effect of these valves, they must be set up using emission test gear and ideally a rolling road - merely turning the pressure up to the maximum level might not produce the desired effect. Fitting one of these valves involves breaking into the high-pressure fuel line, which is potentially dangerous for the inexperienced - also, if the valve is poorly fitted (or the fuel lines are in poor condition), you could end up with fuel spraying out under pressure onto a hot engine. Make sure you know what you're doing - anything involving petrol requires talent - and watch carefully for any sign of fuel leakage after fitting, even if this is done by a professional.

No quicker but it looks nice

Looks are just as important as performance. No hot hatch is 'finished' without making it look sweet. Details to the engine bay as well as your interior and exterior mods are an important factor, especially if you were thinking about getting your motor featured in top magazines. Everyone does it, and you're next.

First up - try cleaning the engine, for flip's sake! How do you expect to emulate the show-stopping cars if your gearbox is covered in grot? Get busy with the degreaser (Gunk's a good bet), then get the hosepipe out. You can take it down to the local jetwash if you like, but remember your mobile - if you get carried away with the high-power spray, you might find the car won't start afterwards!

When it's all dry (and running again), you can start in. Get the polish to all the painted surfaces you reasonably can, and don't be afraid to unbolt a few of the simpler items to gain better access. We're assuming you've already fitted your induction kit, but if not, these nicely do away with a load of ugly plastic airbox/air cleaner and trunking, and that rusted-out exhaust manifold cover, in favour of decent-looking product. Take off the rocker cover, and paint it to match your chosen scheme (heat-resistant paint is a must, really, such as brake caliper paint), set off with a funky oil filler cap. A strut brace is a tasty underbonnet feature, especially chromed. Braided hose covers (or coloured hose sets), ally battery covers and bottles, mirror panels - all give the underbonnet a touch of glamour.

You's a hose

Importante!
If you're removing coolant hoses, feel them up first (oo-er) to make sure they're cold. Have a bowl ready to catch the coolant in (antifreeze is poisonous despite its sweet smell, and will make a mess of your paintwork if you douse the engine bay and front wings with it!). Also, don't forget to top-up the coolant level before heading out.

Importante !
If you're planning to remove any fuel lines, disconnect the hoses very carefully - have some rags wrapped around the pipes, so you don't spray high-pressure fuel everywhere.

01 First, decide which hoses you're going to paint, then work out how to remove them. We can't show you how to remove every single hose, so for more info, refer to the Haynes Punto manual. Always do the biggest first - and they don't get much bigger than the air inlet duct. Start by prising away the spring clip from the breather hose that feeds into the inlet duct.

02 Then prise away the second spring clip that secures the inlet hose to the inlet manifold. The spring clips will be useless after you have removed them, so you'll have to find yourself two Jubilee clips the right size to use when refitting the painted hose.

Remove the hose from the engine - being an air hose, it's not full of anything dangerous, like fuel, power steering fluid, or hot **03** coolant. We like this hose.

It's now time for some intense cleaning treatment. This hose is a bit of a beast to clean, as it has so many grooves and indentations. The best way to clean it is with a paintbrush and lots of degreaser. The pipe must be totally free of any silicone, grease or dirt, or your paint won't stick. Try not to **04** damage the rubber hose by scrubbing at it too hard.

MHW's Tube-It hose paint has been specially developed to stick to rubber surfaces, so is ideal for engine bay hoses which, otherwise, would have to remain boring in black. It only comes in small aerosols, so it may not go as far as you'd like, but you should be able to cover most **05** engine bays with two cans.

Suspend the hose on a piece of wire from up high, put plenty of newspaper down to protect the floor, and spray the hose. Apply the paint in two or three light layers until the coverage on the hose is even, taking care not to encourage paint runs through applying too much paint. Make sure the paint's totally dry **06** before refitting the hose.

Braiding hoses

01 First step is to remove your chosen hose. If supplies of braiding are limited, go for the hoses at the top of the engine first, then the ones underneath you can't see won't matter so much. You'll either find spring-type clips, best released using pliers, or one-shot clips which you destroy during removal. Make sure you've got a supply of new Jubilee clips available, just in case.

02 If the hose is stuck, be careful how you free it, or you could snap the pipe stub underneath (some are only plastic). This sort of thing can really ruin your day. Careful prising with a screwdriver is usually enough to loosen a stubborn hose end.

03 Unroll your braiding, check the length against your freshly-removed hose . . .

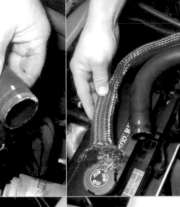

08 . . . before trimming off the excess braiding (and not the hose).

09 Slide a new Jubilee clip over the braiding at one end, then slip one of the coloured end fittings over the clip.

10 Repeat this process at the other end of your chosen hose, and it'll be ready to fit back on.

04 . . . and trim it roughly to length - you might need something heftier than scissors for this.

05 Now expand the braiding to the right size using a suitable blunt object. Like a screwdriver handle, we mean - what were you thinking of?

06 Once the braiding's roughly the right size, you can slip your pipe in (lovely). Smooth out the braiding round the bends, as it tends to gather up and look naff otherwise . . .

07 . . . then (and this bit's optional, but it worked well for us) wrap round a little insulating tape - we had some colour-coded red stuff lying about - to tidy the end . . .

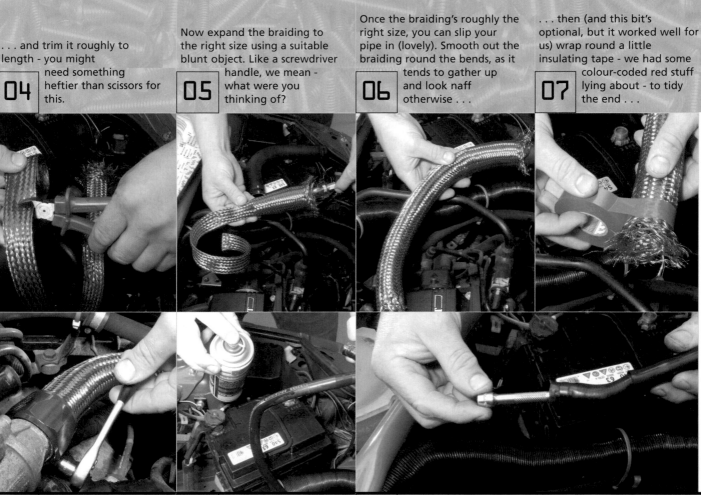

11 When you're sure the hose is fully onto its fitting, tighten the hose clip securely to avoid embarrassing leakage. If any of the end fittings rattle annoyingly, you can put a stop to it by packing the fittings with silicone.

12 If you've got an awkward (kinky) hose to do, make life easier for yourself by spraying on a little rubber lubricant before trying to slip the braiding on . . .

13 . . . and use something like a screwdriver (or a socket extension piece) to straighten out those bends while you're fitting.

Importante !
If you're planning to remove any fuel lines, disconnect the hoses very carefully - have some rags wrapped around the pipes, so you don't spray high-pressure fuel everywhere.

Silicon heaven

All Puntos have an engine management system with a 'computer' at its heart, known as the ECU, or Electronic Control Unit. The ECU contains several computer chips, at least one of which has programmed onto it the preferred fuel/air mixture and ignition advance setting for any given engine speed or load - this information is known as a computer 'map', and the system refers to it constantly while the car's being driven. Obviously, with the current trend towards fuel economy and reducing harmful exhaust emissions, the values in this 'map' are set, well, conservatively, let's say (read 'boring'). With a little tweaking - like richening-up the mixture, say - the engine can be made to produce more power, or response will be improved, or both. At the expense of the environment. Whatever.

Companies like Superchips offer replacement computer chips which feature a computer map where driveability and performance are given priority over outright economy (although the company claims that, under certain conditions, even fuel economy can be better, with their products). The GT was made for chipping, and can show gains of 30 bhp or more from chipping alone. While a chip like this does offer proven power gains on its own, it's obviously best to combine a chip with other enhancements, and to have the whole lot set up at the same time. By the time you've fitted an induction kit, four-branch manifold, big-bore pipe, and maybe even a fast-road cam, adding a chip is the icing on the cake - chipping an already-modified motor will liberate even more horses, or at least combine it with majorly-improved response. Fiat tuning specialists are best placed to advise you on the most effective tuning mods.

Chipping is about the best way to extract more horses if your Punto runs on oil, not petrol. Modern turbo-diesel engine management systems control all aspects of fuelling, as you'd expect, but they also control the turbo boost. The more modern your TD is, the more there is to play with, and the more to be gained. Chipping a petrol engine can mean an extra 10 bhp, but turbo-diesels can give three times that gain, from a chip alone - and still with sensible fuel economy.

Another feature programmed into the ECU is a rev limiter, which cuts the ignition (or fuel) progressively when the pre-set rev limit is reached. Most replacement chips have the rev limiter reset higher, or removed altogether. Not totally sure this is a good thing - if the engine's not maintained properly (low oil level, cambelt changes neglected), removing the rev limiter and running beyond the red line would be a quick way to kill it. But a well-maintained engine with rally cam(s) fitted could rev off the clock, if the ECU would let it, so maybe not a bad thing after all...

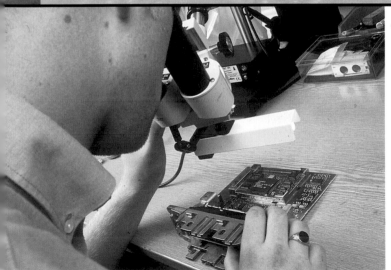

Now the bad news

Chipping is often thought of as an easy, 'no-tell' route to increased performance and driveability - usually, the ECU is well-buried inside the car, so who's gonna know?* Needless to say, the insurance companies have been wise to this trick for a long time. A sure way to tell whether any 'performance' product does what it says on the tin is to see what it'll do to your premium - telling them you're fitting a sports ROM chip will cost. Big-time. But, in the event of a claim, if they suspect your car's been 'chipped', rest assured, they will make efforts to find out, because if you haven't told them about it, it means they save on paying out. What's an insurance assessor's salary for one day, compared to the thousands you could be claiming in case of an accident or theft? Do it by all means, but at least be honest.

*This isn't so on the Punto - the ECU's clearly on display under the bonnet.

Engine tuning

So you've done the filter/induction kit and exhaust box - what's next, short of going for a complete engine swap?

If you've got a sports back box, try a performance exhaust manifold up front - or better still, a full 'cat-back' system for the best gains. Your Punto is, of course, being strangled all the time you're driving. By a cat - how embarrassing is that? There's the option of a de-cat pipe, which does away with the power-sapping catalytic converter at a stroke, freeing-up as many as 10 or 15 horses on the way (but remember the car's not MOT-able with one of these fitted, so isn't strictly legal for use on the road).

A new camshaft's often a juicy way to pep up a standard motor. Standard cams are pretty good these days, but a fast road cam will still give you more top-end (possibly, right at the very top-end, with nothing much below that). Once the ECU rev limiter's been disabled (by chipping), swap the cam(s) and you should see more power further up the rev range. Treat your Punto to a skimmed, gas-flowed, big-valve cylinder head as well, and it'll really start to percolate.

The GT Turbo is obviously the most tuneable Punto, with chipping a favourite first mod. Programmable chips are the best investment if your engine tuning project is likely to be a 'work in progress' - the chip parameters can be changed to match any other mods you make to the motor. After that, we're into hybrid turbos (bigger-capacity, but still spinning-up fast enough to avoid too much lag), water injection (lowers combustion temperatures, stops pinking), and cylinder head mods, possibly including a fast road cam. Turbo engines are also well-suited to a touch of nitrous. It's important, especially on the GT, not to sacrifice driveability too much in your quest for ultimate power - for road use, at least.

Engine **swaps**

Most young Punto owners wait 'til they've built up some no-claims bonus on their insurance, and go for a bigger Fiat engine. Why throw shedloads of cash modding a weenie Fiat engine, when lots less money spent on fitting a new motor could buy you the same power, with room left for tuning?

If you've "only" got a 1.1 litre lump, a swap for the 1.2 16-valver from a Sporting will make a useful difference, as would transplanting the earlier 90 Sporting 1.6 engine. The ultimate, of course, is the GT Turbo engine swap. Nuff said.

And finally

And finally tonight - the bad news. Any major engine mods means telling those nice suits who work for your insurance company, and it's likely they'll insist on a full engineer's report (these aren't especially expensive - look one up in the Yellow Pages, under *'Garage Services'* or *'Vehicle Inspection'*).

Exhausts

It's gotta be done, hasn't it? Your rusty old exhaust lacks the girth to impress, and doesn't so much growl as miaow. Don't be a wimp and fit an exhaust trim - they'll fool nobody who really knows, and they certainly won't add to your aural pleasure (oo-er). Sort yourself out a decent back box upgrade, and even a timid 1.1 Punto can begin to cut it at the cruise.

What a back box won't do on its own is increase engine power - although it'll certainly sound like it has, provided you choose the right one, and fit it properly. Check when you're buying that it can be fitted to a standard system - you'll probably need something called a reducing sleeve for a decent fit, which is a section of pipe designed to bridge the difference between your small-diameter pipe and the larger-diameter silencer. Try and measure your standard pipe as accurately as possible, or you'll have major problems trying to get a decent seal between the old and new bits - don't assume that exhaust paste will sort everything out, because it won't.

Fashion has even entered the aftermarket exhaust scene, with different rear pipe designs going in and out of style. Everyone's done the upswept twin-pipe 'DTM' style pipes, while currently the trend in single pipes is massive Jap-style round exits, or fat oval (or twin-oval) designs. If you must have the phattest Punto on the

Know your enemy - this is what your cat looks like inside. Is it any wonder they restrict gas flow?

block, you can't beat a twin-exit system (from someone like Powerflow), even though it'll probably mean losing your spare wheel in the fitting process. Well, when was the last time you had a puncture? And what are mobiles and breakdown cover for, anyway?

You might need to lightly modify even your standard rear bodywork/bumper to accommodate a bigger rear pipe; if you're going for a bodykit later, your back box will have to come off again, so it can be poked through your rear valance/mesh.

You'll see some useful power gains if you go for the complete performance exhaust system (cat-back system), rather than just the back box. Like the factory-fit system, the sports silencer works best combined with the front pipe and manifold it was designed for! Performance four-branch manifolds alone can give very useful power gains. Watch what you buy, though - cheap exhaust manifolds which crack for a pastime are not unknown, and many aftermarket systems need careful fitting and fettling before you'll stop it resonating or banging away underneath. A sports rear box alone shouldn't attract an increased insurance premium, but a full system probably will.

All Puntos (even the GT) are lumbered with a catalytic converter (or 'cat'), which acts like a restrictor in the exhaust, inhibiting the gas flow and sapping some engine power (maybe 5 to 10%). Various specialist exhaust companies market replacement sections which do away with the cat (a 'de-cat pipe'), and get you your power back. Unfortunately, by taking off or disabling the cat, your car won't be able to pass the emissions test at MOT time, so you'll have to 're-convert' the car every 12 months. This means the car's illegal on the road with a de-cat pipe fitted - you'd have no defence for this, if questions were asked at the roadside, and potentially no insurance if the unthinkable happens. Sorry, but we have to say it…

If your Punto has been slammed to the floor, will your big new sports system be leaving behind a trail of sparks as it scrapes along the deck? Shouldn't do, if it's been properly fitted, but will the local multi-storey be out-of-bounds for your Punto, from now on? And - pub trivia moment - you can actually be done for causing damage to the highway, if your exhaust's dragging. Well, great.

You probably couldn't give a stuff if your loud system's a very loud major public nuisance, but will that loud pipe start interfering with your sound system? If you rack up many motorway miles, you might find the constant drone of a loud pipe gets to be a real pain on a long trip, too…

Fitting a **cat-back exhaust**

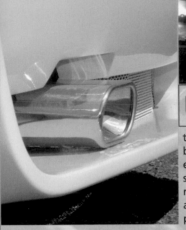

01 The first job is to remove the standard exhaust from behind the catalytic converter (cat-back). Begin by undoing the exhaust clamp at the engine-side of the centre box. To help remove the rusty clamp, give it a good spray with a rust-penetrating lubricant.

02 Once the clamp's been removed, the pipes need to be separated. Some persuasion with a hammer may be necessary (swearing optional). If you can get any twist on the pipes, this also helps separate rusted-together sections. Just get the pipes loose for now - leave them joined together.

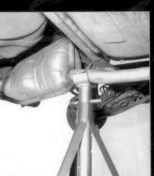

03 Next, pop an axle stand under the back box to support its weight when the exhaust is unhooked from the mounting rubbers . . .

04 . . . because that's next. There are two in total, one between the centre and back box (we'll call it the central mounting), the other on the exit side of the back box (the rear mountIng). A little more lube spray to help things along, then prise the rubber mountings off using a flat-bladed screwdriver.

05 Now the front joint can be separated . . .

06 . . . and the whole rusty old system can be lowered out and removed from car.

07 That's more like it - some shiny exhaust bits at last. Take the new centre box and try it for size . . .

08 . . . noting that, if your Punto's like ours, you'll have an alignment pin on the old pipe, which should locate in one of the slots on the new centre box pipe.

09 A new exhaust clamp can be fitted now (the old one's probably had it, anyway). The clamp sits behind the alignment pin, which acts as a barrier keeping the clamp in place.

10 Give the central rubber mounting a squirt of lube before trying to ease the new mounting bracket into place.

11 The back box is now ready to be offered into place. When you're happy with the position of the box, support it in place using an axle stand.

12 Our box came with a wrap-round support bracket, which you slide it over the box, into place.

13 As before, give the area a good squirt of lube, then ease the support mounting bracket into place on the rear rubber mounting. Once it's on, the axle stand can be taken away.

14 Tighten the clamp bolt on the rear box support bracket, and you're nearly finished.

15 Finally, fit and tighten the exhaust clamp. Back boxes and rear bumpers can be a problem area on Puntos (Peco have just re-designed their back boxes to be more Punto-friendly). Depending on what style of exhaust and rear bumper you've chosen, typically, a little chopping and re-shaping of glassfibre may be needed for perfection - speak nicely to your bodyshop.

14 Safety and tools

Safety

We all know that working on your car can be dangerous - and we're not talking about the danger of losing your street cred by fitting naff alloys or furry dice! Okay, so you'd be hard-pushed to injure yourself fitting some cool floor mats or a tax disc holder, but tackle more-serious mods, and you could be treading dangerous ground. Let's be honest - we have to put this safety section in to cover ourselves, but now it's in, it would be nice if you read it...

Burning/scalding

The only way you'll really burn yourself is if your car's just been running - avoid this, and you won't get burned. Easy, eh? Otherwise, you risk burns from any hot parts of the engine (and especially the exhaust - if you've got one, the cat runs very hot), or from spilling hot coolant if you undo the radiator hoses or filler cap, as you might when you're braiding hoses.

Fire

Sadly, there's several ways your car could catch fire, when you think about it. You've got a big tank full of fuel (and other flammable liquids about, like brake fluid), together with electrics - some of which run to very high voltages. If you smoke too, this could be even worse for your health than you thought.

a Liquid fuel is flammable. Fuel vapour can explode - don't smoke, or create any kind of spark, if there's fuel vapour (fuel smell) about.

b Letting fuel spill onto a hot engine is dangerous, but brake fluid spills go up even more readily. Respect is due with brake fluid, which also attacks paintwork and plastics - wash off with water.

c Fires can also be started by careless modding involving the electrical system. It's possible to overload (and overheat) existing wiring by tapping off too many times for new live feeds. Not insulating bare wires or connections can lead to short-circuits, and the sparks or overheated wiring which results can start a fire. Always investigate any newly-wired-in kit which stops working, or which keeps blowing fuses - those wires could already be smouldering...

Crushing

Having your car land on top of you is no laughing matter, and it's a nasty accident waiting to happen if you risk using dodgy old jacks, bricks, and other means of lifting/supporting your car. Please don't.

Your standard vehicle jack is for emergency roadside use only - a proper trolley jack and a set of axle stands won't break the overdraft, and might save broken bones. Don't buy a cheap trolley jack, and don't expect a well-used secondhand one to be perfect, either - when the hydraulic seals start to fail, a trolley jack will drop very fast; this is why you should always have decent stands in place under the car as well.

Steering, suspension & brakes

Screwing up any one of these on your car, through badly-fitted mods, could land you and others in hospital or worse. Nuff said? It's always worth getting a mate, or a friendly garage, to check over what you've just fitted (or even what you've just had fitted, in some cases - not all "pro" fitters are perfect!). Pay attention to tightening vital nuts and bolts properly - buy or borrow a torque wrench.

To be absolutely sure, take your newly-modded machine to a friendly MOT tester (if there is such a thing) - this man's your ultimate authority on safety, after all. Even if he's normally a pain once a year, he could save your life. Think it over.

Even properly-fitted mods can radically alter the car's handling - and not always for the better. Take a few days getting used to how the car feels before showing off.

Wheels

Don't take liberties fitting wheels. Make sure the wheels have the right stud/bolt hole pattern for your car, and that the wheel nuts/bolts are doing their job. Bolts which are too long might catch on your brakes (especially rear drums) - too short, and, well, the wheels are just waiting to fall off. Not nice. Also pay attention to the bolt heads or wheel nuts - some are supposed to have large tapered washers fitted, to locate properly in the wheel. If the nuts/bolts "pull through" the wheel when tightened, the wheel's gonna fall off, isn't it?

Asbestos

Only likely to be a major worry when working on, or near, your brakes. That black dust that gets all over your alloys comes from your brake pads, and it may contain asbestos. Breathing in asbestos dust can lead to a disease called asbestosis (inflammation of the lungs - very nasty indeed), so try not to inhale brake dust when you're changing your pads or discs.

Airbags

Unless you run into something at high speed, the only time an airbag will enter your life is when you change your steering wheel for something more sexy, and have to disable the airbag in the process. Pay attention to all the precautionary advice given in our text, and you'll have no problems.

One more thing - don't tap into the airbag wiring to run any extra electrical kit. Any mods to the airbag circuit could set it off unexpectedly.

Exhaust gases

Even on cars with cats, exhaust fumes are still potentially lethal. Don't work in an unventilated garage with the engine running. When fitting new exhaust bits, be sure that there's no gas leakage from the joints. When modifying in the tailgate area, note that exhaust gas can get sucked into the car through badly-fitting tailgate seals/joints (or even through your rear arches, if they've been trimmed so much there's holes into the car).

Tools

In writing this book, we've assumed you already have a selection of basic tools - screwdrivers, socket set, spanners, hammer, sharp knife, power drill. Any unusual extra tools you might need are mentioned in the relevant text. Torx and Allen screws are often found on trim panels, so a set of keys of each type is a wise purchase.

From a safety angle, always buy the best tools you can afford - or if you must use cheap ones, remember that they can break under stress or unusual usage (and we've all got the busted screwdrivers to prove it!).

DO Wear goggles when using power tools.

DO Keep loose clothing/long hair away from moving engine parts.

DO Take off watches and jewellery when working on electrics.

DO Keep the work area tidy - stops accidents and losing parts.

DON'T Rush a job, or take stupid short-cuts.

DON'T Use the wrong tools for the job, or ones which don't fit.

DON'T Let kids or pets play around your car when you're working.

DON'T Work entirely alone under a car that's been jacked up.

Legal modding?
No such thing!!

The harsh & painful truth

The minute you start down the road to a modified motor, you stand a good chance of being in trouble with the Man. It seems like there's almost nothing worthwhile you can do to your car, without breaking some sort of law. So the answer's not to do it at all, then? Well, no, but let's keep it real.

There's this bunch of vehicle-related regulations called Construction & Use. It's a huge set of books, used by the car manufacturers and the Department of Transport among others, and it sets out in black and white all the legal issues that could land you in trouble. It's the ultimate authority for modifying, in theory. But few people (and even fewer policemen) know all of it inside-out, and it's forever being updated and revised, so it's not often enforced to the letter at the roadside - just in court. Despite the existence of C & U, in trying to put together any guide to the law and modifying, it quickly becomes clear that almost everything's a "grey area", with no-one prepared to go on record and say what is okay to modify and what's not. Well, brilliant. So if there's no fixed rules (in the real world), how are you meant to live by them? In the circumstances, all we can promise to do is help to make sense of nonsense…

Avoiding roadside interviews

Why do some people get pulled all the time, and others hardly ever? It's often all about attitude. We'd all like to be free to drive around "in yer face", windows down, system full up, loud exhaust bellowing, sparks striking, tyres squealing - but - nothing is a bigger "come-on" to the boys in blue than "irresponsible" driving like this. Rest assured, if your motor's anywhere near fully sorted, the coppers will find something they can nick you for, when they pull you over - it's a dead cert. Trying not to wind them up too much before this happens (and certainly not once you're stopped) will make for an easier life. There's showing off, and then there's taking the pee. Save it for the next cruise.

The worst thing from your point of view is that, once you've been stopped, it's down to that particular copper's judgement as to whether your car's illegal. If he/she's having a bad day anyway, smart-mouthing-off isn't gonna help your case at all. If you can persuade him/her that you're at least taking on board what's being said, you might be let off with a warning. If it goes further, you'll be reported for an offence - while this doesn't mean you'll end up being prosecuted for it, it ain't good. Some defects (like worn tyres) will result in a so-called "seven-day wonder", which usually means you have to fix whatever's deemed wrong, maybe get the car inspected, and present yourself with the proof at a police station, inside seven days, or face prosecution.

If you can manage to drive reasonably sensibly when the law's about, and can ideally show that you've tried to keep your car legal when you get questioned, you stand a much better chance of enjoying your relationship with your modded beast. This guide is intended to help you steer clear of the more obvious things you could get pulled for. By reading it, you might even be able to have an informed, well-mannered discussion about things legal with the next officer of the law you meet at the side of the road. As in: "Oh really, officer? I was not aware of that. Thank you for pointing it out." Just don't argue with them, that's all…

Documents

The first thing you'll be asked to produce. If you're driving around without tax, MOT or insurance, we might as well stop now, as you won't be doing much more driving of anything after just one pull.

Okay, so you don't normally carry all your car-related documents with you - for safety, you've got them stashed carefully at home, haven't you? But carrying photocopies of your licence, MOT and insurance certificate is a good idea. While they're not legally-binding absolute proof, producing these in a roadside check might mean you don't have to produce the real things at a copshop later in the week. Shows a certain responsibility, and confidence in your own legality on the road, too. In some parts of the country, it's even said to be a good idea to carry copies of any receipts for your stereo gear - if there's any suspicion about it being stolen (surely not), some coppers have been known to confiscate it (or the car it's in) on the spot!

Number plates

One of the simplest mods, and one of the easiest to spot (and prove) if you're a copper. Nowadays, any changes made to the standard approved character font (such as italics or fancy type), spacing, or size of the plate constitutes an offence. Remember too that if you've moved the rear plate from its original spot (like from the tailgate recess, during smoothing) it still has to be properly lit at night. You're unlikely to even buy an illegal plate now, as the companies making them are also liable for prosecution if you get stopped. It's all just something else to blame on speed cameras - plates have to be easy for them to shoot, and modding yours suggests you're trying to escape a speeding conviction (well, who isn't?).

Getting pulled for an illegal plate is for suckers - you're making it too easy for them. While this offence only entails a small fine and confiscation of the plates, you're drawing unwelcome police attention to the rest of your car. Not smart. At all.

Sunstrips and tints

The sunstrip is now an essential item for any modded motor, but telling Mr Plod you had to fit one is no defence if you've gone a bit too far. The sunstrip should not be so low down the screen that it interferes with your ability to see out. Is this obvious? Apparently not. As a guide, if the strip's so low your wiper(s) touch it, it's too low. Don't try fitting short wiper blades to get round this - the police aren't as stupid as that, and you could get done for wipers that don't clear a sufficient area of the screen. Push it so far, and no further!

Window tinting is a trickier area. It seems you can have up to a 25% tint on a windscreen, and up to 30% on all other glass - but how do you measure this? Er. And what do you do if your glass is tinted to start with? Er, probably nothing. Of course you can buy window film in various "darknesses", from not-very-dark to "ambulance-black", but being able to buy it does not make it legal for road use (most companies cover themselves by saying "for show use only"). Go for just a light smoke on the side and rear glass, and you'd have to be unlucky to get done for it. If you must fit really dark tints, you're safest doing the rear side windows only.

Some forces now have a light meter to test light transmission through glass at the roadside - fail this, and it's a big on-the-spot fine.

Single wiper conversion

Not usually a problem, and certainly not worth a pull on its own, but combine a big sunstrip with a short wiper blade, and you're just asking for trouble. Insufficient view of the road ahead. There's also the question of whether it's legal to have the arm parking vertically, in the centre of the screen, as it obscures your vision. Probably not legal, then - even if it looks cool. Unfortunately, the Man doesn't do cool.

Lights

Lights of all kinds have to be one of the single biggest problem areas in modifying, and the police are depressingly well-informed. Most people make light mods a priority, whether it's Morette conversions for headlights or Lexus-style rear clusters. If they fit alright, and work, what's the problem?

First off, don't bother with any lights which aren't fully UK-legal - it's just too much hassle. Being "E-marked" only makes them legal in Europe, and most of our Euro-chums drive on the right. One of our project cars ended up with left-hand-drive rear clusters, and as a result, had no rear reflectors and a rear foglight on the wrong side (should be on the right). Getting stopped for not having rear reflectors would be a bit harsh, but why risk it, even to save a few quid?

Once you've had any headlight mods done (other than light brows) always have the beam alignment checked - it's part of the MOT, after all. The same applies to any front fogs or spots you've fitted (the various points of law involved here are too many to mention - light colour, height, spacing, operation with main/dipped headlights - ask at an MOT centre before fitting, and have them checked out after fitting).

If Plod's really having a bad day, he might even question the legality of your new blue headlight bulbs - are they too powerful? Keeping the bulb packaging in the glovebox might be a neat solution here (60/55W max).

Many modders favour spraying rear light clusters to make them look trick, as opposed to replacing them - but there's trouble in store here, too. One of the greyest of grey areas is - how much light tinting is too much? The much-talked-about but not-often-seen "common sense" comes into play here. Making your lights so dim that they're reduced to a feeble red/orange glow is pretty dim itself. If you're spraying, only use proper light-tinting spray, and not too many coats of that. Colour-coding lights with ordinary spray paint is best left to a pro sprayer or bodyshop (it can be done by mixing lots of lacquer with not much paint, for instance). Tinted lights are actually more of a problem in daylight than at night, so check yours while the sun's out.

Lastly, two words about neons. Oh, dear. It seems that neons of all kinds have now been deemed illegal for road use (and that's

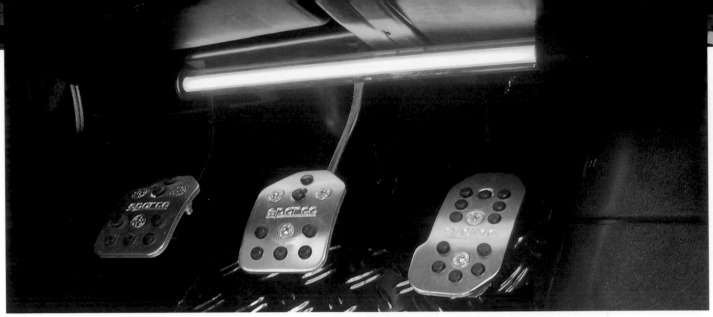

interior ones as well as exteriors, which have pretty much always been a no-no). If you fit neons inside, make sure you rig in a switch so you can easily turn them off when the law arrives - or don't drive around with them on (save it for when you're parked up). Distracts other road users, apparently.

ICE

Jungle massive, or massive public nuisance? The two sides of the ICE argument in a nutshell. If you've been around the modding scene for any length of time, you'll already know stories of people who've been done for playing car stereos too loud. Seems some local authorities now have by-laws concerning "music audible from outside a vehicle", and hefty fines if you're caught. Even where this isn't the case, and assuming a dB meter isn't on hand to prove the offence of "excessive noise", the police can still prosecute for "disturbing the peace" - on the basis of one officer's judgement of the noise level. If a case is proved, you could lose your gear. Whoops. Seems we're back to "do it - but don't over-do it" again. If you really want to demo your system, pick somewhere a bit less public (like a quiet trading estate, after dark) or go for safety in numbers (at a cruise).

Big alloys/tyres

One of the first things to go on any lad's car, sexy alloys are right at the heart of car modifying. So what'll interest the law?

Well, the first thing every copper's going to wonder is - are the wheels nicked? He'd need a good reason to accuse you, but this is another instance where having copies of receipts might prove useful.

Otherwise, the wheels mustn't rub on, or stick out from, the arches - either of these will prove to be a problem if you get stopped. And you don't need to drive a modded motor to get done for having bald tyres…

Lowered suspension

Of course you have to lower your car, to have any hope of street cred. But did you know it's actually an offence to cause damage to the road surface, if your car's so low (or your mates so lardy) that it grounds out? Apparently so! Never mind what damage it might be doing to your exhaust, or the brake/fuel lines under the car - you can actually get done for risking damage to the road. Well, great. What's the answer? Once you've lowered the car, load it up with your biggest mates, and test it over roads you normally use - or else find a route into town that avoids all speed bumps. If you've got coilovers, you'll have an easier time tuning out the scraping noises.

Remember that your new big-bore exhaust or backbox must be hung up well enough that it doesn't hit the deck, even if you haven't absolutely slammed your car on the floor. At night, leaving a trail of sparks behind is a bit of a giveaway…

Exhausts

One of the easiest-to-fit performance upgrades, and another essential item if you want to be taken seriously on the street. Unless your chosen pipe/system is just too damn loud, you'd be very unlucky to get stopped for it, but if you will draw attention this way, you could be kicking yourself later.

For instance - have you in fact fitted a home-made straight-through pipe, to a car which used to have a "cat"? By drawing Plod's attention with that extra-loud system, he could then ask you to get the car's emissions tested - worse, you could get pulled for a "random" roadside emissions check. Fail this (and you surely will), and you could be right in the brown stuff. Even if you re-convert the car back to stock for the MOT, you'll be illegal on the road (and therefore without insurance) whenever your loud pipe's on. Still sound like fun, or would you be happier with just a back box?

It's also worth mentioning that your tailpipe mustn't stick out beyond the very back of the car, or in any other way which might be dangerous to pedestrians. Come on - you were a ped once!

Bodykits

The popular bodykits for the UK market have all passed the relevant tests, and are fully-approved for use on the specific vehicles they're intended for. As long as you haven't messed up fitting a standard kit, you should be fine, legally-speaking. The trouble starts when you do your own little mods and tweaks, such as bodging on that huge whale-tail spoiler or front air dam/splitter - it can be argued in some cases that these aren't appropriate on safety grounds, and you can get prosecuted. If any bodywork is fitted so it obscured your lights, or so badly attached that a strong breeze might blow it off, you can see their point. At least there's no such thing as Style Police. Not yet, anyway.

Seats and harnesses

Have to meet the UK safety standards, and must be securely bolted in. That's about it. It should be possible to fasten and release any seat belt or harness with one hand. Given that seat belts are pretty important safety features, it's understandable then that the police don't like to see flimsy alloy rear strut braces used as seat harness mounting points. Any other signs of bodging will also spell trouble. It's unlikely they'd bother with a full safety inspection at the roadside, but they could insist on a full MOT test/engineer's report inside 7 days. It's your life.

While we're on the subject of crash safety, the police also don't like to see sub boxes and amps just lying on the carpet, where the back seat used to be - if it's not anchored down, where are these items gonna end up, in a big shunt? Embedded in you, possibly?

Other mods

We'll never cover everything else here, and the law's always changing anyway, so we're fighting a losing battle in a book like this, but here goes with some other legalistic points we've noted on the way:

a It's illegal to remove side repeaters from front wings, even to create the ultimate smoothed/flushed motor. Sorry.

b All except the most prehistoric cars must have at least one rear foglight. If there's only one, it must be fitted on the right. We've never heard of anyone getting stopped for it, but you must also have a pair of rear reflectors. If your rear clusters ain't got 'em, can you get trendy ones? Er, no.

c Fuel filler caps have to be fitted so there's no danger of fuel spillage, or of excess fumes leaking from the top of the filler neck. This means using an appropriate petrol-resistant sealer (should be supplied in the kit). Oh, and not bodging the job in general seems a good idea. Unlikely to attract a pull, though.

d Front doors have to retain a manual means of opening from outside, even if they've been de-locked for remote locking. This means you can't take off the front door handles, usually. It seems that rear door handles can be removed if you like.

e Tailgates have to have some means of opening, even if it's only from inside, once the lock/handle's been removed. We think it's another safety thing - means of escape in a crash, and all that.

f You have to have at least one exterior mirror, and it must be capable of being adjusted somehow.

g If you fit new fog and spotlights, they actually have to work. No-one fits new lights just for show (or do they?), but if they stop working later when a fuse blows, relay packs up, or the wiring connectors rust up, you'd better fix 'em or remove 'em.

h Pedal extensions must have rubbers fitted on the brake and clutch pedals, and must be spaced sufficiently so there's no chance of hitting two pedals at once. This last bit sounds obvious, but lots of extension sets out there are so hard to fit that achieving this can be rather difficult. Don't get caught out.

i On cars with airbags, if you fit a sports wheel and disconnect the airbag in the process, the airbag warning light will be on permanently. Apart from being annoying, this is also illegal.

j Pace-car strobe lights (or any other flashing lights, apart from indicators) are illegal for road use. Of course.

k Anything else we didn't think of - is probably illegal too. Sorry.

Any questions? Try the MOT Helpline (0845 6005977). Yes, really.

Thanks to Andrew Dare of the Vehicle Inspectorate, Exeter, for his help in steering us through this minefield!

Thanks to:

We gratefully acknowledge all the help and advice offered from the following suppliers, without whom, etc, etc. Many of those credited below went way beyond the call of duty to help us produce this book - you know who you are. Cheers, guys! Roll the credits...

ABC Design Autostyling Ltd
(AutoArt & MHW)
www.abcdesignltd.com

Auto Inparts Ltd
(accessories)
01525 382713

Autotint Design
(bonnet vent)
0113 289 1500
www.autotintdesign.com

Britannia Cars
(Morette headlights)
01442 490700

Brown & Geeson
(Momo accessories)
01268 764411
www.brownandgeeson.com

Cobra Seats
(seats and harnesses)
01952 684020
www.cobraseats.com

Cooper Avon Tyres
01225 703101
www.coopertire.com

Dash Dynamics (dash kit)
0870 127 0003
www.dashdynamics.co.uk

Demon Tweeks (accessories)
01978 664466
www.demon-tweeks.co.uk

Draper Tools (tools)
023 8026 6355
www.draper.co.uk

ESP Design Ltd
01621 869866
www.espdesign.co.uk

Eurostyling (Folia Tec)
01908 324950
www.eurostyling.com

Halfords
08457 626 625

Haynes Motor Museum
(paint and bodywork)
01963 440804
www.haynesmotormuseum.com

Microscan Alarms
www.microscanalarms.co.uk

A & I Peco (exhaust box)
0151 647 6041
www.peco.co.uk

Pipercross
(induction systems)
01604 494945
www.pipercross.com

ProSport UK Ltd
(Body kit)
08707 477677
www.prosport.uk.com

Red Dot Racing
(brake discs & pads)
020 8888 2354
www.reddotracing.co.uk

Richbrook
(sport auto accessories)
020 8543 7111
www.richbrook.co.uk

Ripspeed at Halfords
0845 609 1259

Safety Devices
(fire extinguisher)
01353 724201
www.safetydevices.co.uk

SPAX
01869 244771
www.spaxperformance.com

SW Autodesign
(Momo wheels)
0161 366 8536
www.swautodesign.com

Venom Motorsport Ltd
(number plate recess)
01245 814444
www.venommotorsport.com

A special thank you to:
Bryn Musselwhite

Editorial Director	Matthew Minter
Designer	Simon Larkin
Page Build	James Robertson
Workshop	Paul Buckland Pete Trott
Editor	Ian Barnes
Project Co-ordinator	Carole Turk
Production Control	Kevin Heals

Haynes Car Manuals

Haynes Car Service and Repair Manuals are available from car accessory retailers.
For further information or to find your nearest stockist, call **01963 442030** or visit **www.haynes.co.uk**